3-15-60

THE GOSPEL OF THE INCARNATION

BOOKS BY GEORGE S. HENDRY

Published by The Westminster Press

The Gospel of the Incarnation
The Holy Spirit in Christian Theology

THE GOSPEL OF THE INCARNATION

by

George S. Hendry

Philadelphia

THE WESTMINSTER PRESS

Library of Congress Catalog Card No.: 58–5021

PRINTED IN THE UNITED STATES OF AMERICA

To

S. M. H.

April 6, 1932 – April 6, 1957

Contents

Foreword

THE FOLLOWING pages represent the Croall Lectures that were delivered in New College, Edinburgh, in October, 1951. The delay in publication so far beyond the stipulated period of one year has been due, partly to the pressure of other tasks, but principally to my desire to devote further study and reflection to the theme. Advantage has also been taken of opportunities to present the argument to various audiences, from whose comments and criticisms I trust it has benefited.

The incarnation is a subject that has not received much attention in the theology of the Reformed tradition, and some may be disposed to regard a book that is concerned with it as an incursion into a peculiar preserve of Anglican theology. It is the main contention of the book that this kind of preoccupation with single elements of the gospel, such as the incarnation or the atonement, to the relative neglect of others, has been the bane of Christendom and has much to do with our unhappy divisions. The more specific thesis, which is advanced here, is that the principal cause of this fragmentation of the gospel has been the neglect of the incarnate life of Christ, and this in turn is traced to the metaphysical misconstruction of the humanity of Christ in the thought of the early church, as it is enshrined in the second *homo-ousion* of the Chalcedonian Definition. I have tried to show that the meaning of both the incarnation and the atonement must be sought in the life of Christ, if we are to be delivered from extraneous and divisive theories and enabled to recover the wholeness of the gospel. This is the theological task to which the ecumenical movement points.

I wish to express my thanks to the Trustees for the honor

of the invitation to contribute to the distinguished series of the Croall Lectures and for the patience with which they have endured my delinquency in the matter of publication. It is also a pleasure to recall the kindness and hospitality which were shown me by the Principal and Faculty of New College at the time the lectures were delivered. I owe a special debt of gratitude to my friend and colleague, Dr. Hugh T. Kerr, Jr., who generously read the manuscript and suggested a number of improvements.

Princeton, New Jersey

Abbreviations

CR .... *Corpus Reformatorum*

DG .... Harnack, *Lehrbuch der Dogmengeschichte,* 4th edition. Mohr, Tübingen, 1909

ET .... English Translation

KD .... Karl Barth, *Kirchliche Dogmatik.* Zollikon, 1932 ff.

LCC .... Library of Christian Classics. The Westminster Press, 1953 ff.

PG .... Migne, *Patrologia Graeca*

S. T. .... Thomas Aquinas, *Summa Theologica*

WA .... Luther's Works, Weimar Edition

CHAPTER

I

The Fragmentation of the Gospel

THE QUEST for the reunion of Christendom, within the ecumenical movement, has brought to light the significant fact that the causes of our unhappy divisions are not limited to differences on specific controversial issues, but they include also partialities and deficiencies in the apprehension of the gospel, from which no communion is exempt. Concurrent with the divisions of the churches, part cause and part effect, there has been a "general fragmentation of Christian tradition" – the phrase is taken from the Report on the Church prepared by the Theological Commission for the Lund Conference on Faith and Order.[1] This fragmentation is found not only in the doctrine of the church, but it has its roots in what the same Report calls "different conceptions of the mode of the divine action in the world of history, persons, and things," or what we may call, in a word, different conceptions of the gospel. The divisions of the churches correspond to partialities in their views of the basic fact to which they owe their existence. The pursuit of reunion, therefore, must involve, not only the resolution of the familiar points of disagreement, but, as the essential precondition of that, the correction of these partial perspectives and the recovery of the wholeness of the gospel.

The principal way in which this may be looked for is by

[1] *The Church: Report of a Theological Commission on Faith and Order,* p. 10. S. C. M. Press, Ltd., 1951.

renewed study of the Bible, and it is a hopeful sign, as the Faith and Order Report points out, that the revival of Biblical theology, which is apparent in many different parts of Christendom, is opening up roads toward reconciliation. "Theologians have been discovering from the renewed study of the Bible perspectives of truth which they had become inclined to forget; and the theology of the Bible has been found in a number of matters to take us behind some of the familiar antitheses may be partly misleading."[2] Since all churches, except Rome, ascribe to the Bible a unique, or at least a supreme authority, there is real hope that in this way they may be led to a recovery of the wholeness they have lost. The attempt at an ecumenical approach to the gospel in the present work is offered as a contribution to this end.

All churches are agreed that the basis of their life and their message is the gospel of Jesus Christ. Wherein do they disagree? Partly in that they put different interpretations upon specific matters in the gospel, such as the institution of the church, the ministry, and the sacraments. But it is also in large measure because they place different emphases on different parts or aspects of the total gospel of Christ. Each has its attention focused primarily on one side of the picture, and it is relatively blind or indifferent to the others. The estrangement of the churches owes much to these partial perspectives, because, when attention is concentrated unduly on one limited aspect of the gospel, that aspect, not being viewed in the context of the whole gospel, is usually distorted and made to bear a disproportionate weight of significance.

These partialities of perspective are closely related to what Tillich calls the "norms" of theology.[3] He has pointed out that every theological system which uses the Bible as its primary source interprets it in the light of a certain principle, which it

[2] *Op. cit.*, p. 11.

[3] Tillich, *Systematic Theology, I*, pp. 47 ff. University of Chicago Press, 1951.

uses as a criterion or norm. The norm is derived from the Bible in an encounter between the church and the Bible, and it reflects a particular historical situation, a particular view of the human predicament, and a particular type of piety. The most familiar example is the so-called material principle of the Lutheran Reformation, the doctrine of justification by faith; Luther saw in this doctrine the central content of the Biblical revelation, and he used it to regulate his perspective on the gospel and even, as is well known, his estimation of the Biblical writings themselves. Similar norms have been operative explicitly or implicitly at all times.

The diversity of the norms that are employed is manifest not only in the estrangement of the divided churches but also in tensions that are felt within individual churches and traditions. There is a tension of this sort within evangelical Protestantism between two divergent conceptions of the relation between Christians and Christ, which was exposed in a challenging way in the first decade of this century by Wilhelm Herrmann in his widely read book *Communion with God.* There is, on the one hand, the conception of the relation as personal communion with a living and present Lord. Within the last century and a half it has come to appear self-evident to an increasing number of people that such a relation forms the indispensable basis of a living faith. It is proclaimed as such from many pulpits, and it forms the aspiration of many devout Christians. "Do we not then believe that Christ lives and rules? And if we do believe this in real earnest, must we not then suppose that we can commune with him? And if we may have this communion, who would forbid a Christian aspiring to attain the same?"[4] These are the questions of popular piety, according to Herrmann, and they would seem to admit of only one answer. But Herrmann himself refused to give this answer. "We must not be troubled," he wrote, "by hearing it

[4] Herrmann, *Communion with God,* p. 289. Williams and Norgate, 1906.

often said in the church and by Christians whom we cordially esteem, that the most important thing is that every man come into personal relationship with the living Savior and so commune with him"; and he declared roundly, "We cannot speak of a communion with the exalted Christ . . . ; the risen Christ is hidden from us."[5] These statements sounded so astonishing that some of his readers thought Herrmann could not have meant them to be taken seriously.[6] But he was quite serious, and the reason why he took this attitude was that, in his judgment, the type of piety that concentrates on communion with the living Christ tends to give little or no place to a relation of the Christian to the historic work of Christ's incarnate life. The Christian's relation to Christ, he maintained, must be solidly grounded in "the historical event of Christ's life in the real world"; and "the joys of so-called contemplative love to Christ" tend to loose it from its foundation and let it soar in a cloudland of fancy. The danger that Herrmann saw was that the living Christ, to whom this type of piety attaches itself, might become dissociated from the Christ who died; and his contention was that the Christ of history, who is the "real" Christ, must be the focus of evangelical faith and piety.

The conception of a relation of the Christian to the living Christ need not be of the contemplative or mystical type, which Herrmann had chiefly in mind. It may also take the ethical form of an acknowledgment of the living authority and power of Christ. The primitive church confessed its faith in the short formula "Jesus Christ is Lord." To many in modern Christendom the Lordship of Jesus Christ suggests either the reality of his directive control over the lives of those who commit themselves to him, or his sovereign rule over history. In a

[5] *Op. cit.*, p. 291.

[6] William Sanday, for example, wrote: "A great deal may be forgiven to Prof. Herrmann. He so evidently has the root of the matter, and so evidently knows in his own person what communion with God really means." (*Christologies Ancient and Modern*, pp. 107 f., Oxford University Press, 1910.)

time like the present, when the world is beset with confusion and menaced by the pretensions of human power, the thought of the Lordship of Christ has brought comfort and strength to the church. Herrmann would probably not have disputed this. But he might well have pointed to the danger, which is present here too, of abstraction from the " real " Christ. And, indeed, it is doubtful if the Lordship of Christ ever meant merely his ethical authority or his sovereign rule over history to the Christians of the New Testament, and did not always refer first and foremost to the triumphal conclusion of his historic work. This was the center from which it drew its meaning and its power. Christ was, indeed, Lord of their lives and ruler of events, but they knew him as such because his Lordship had been proved in what he had accomplished in his incarnate life. A conception of the Lordship of Christ that does not relate it basically to his saving work is out of harmony with the New Testament.

The contrasted conception belongs to orthodox Protestantism. Here the saving work of Christ holds the central place, and the Christian life is construed accordingly, not in terms of personal communion with a living Lord, but in terms of personal appropriation of the salvation he wrought. The emphasis is not on the presence of the living Christ but on the availability of the benefits of his work. This emphasis received classical expression at the time of the Reformation in Melanchthon's famous words, " To know Christ means to know his benefits." [7] " Benefits " became the key word for the Protestant understanding of the gospel; and the constitutive Christian experience was the appropriation of them, especially justification by faith. This is well illustrated in John Wesley's account of his conversion experience: what caused his heart to become " strangely warmed " was not an experience of communion

[7] (*Hoc est Christum cognoscere, beneficia eius cognoscere*), *Loci Communes* (1521), *CR*, 21, 85. Melanchthon, of course, was pointing a different contrast, viz., with a speculative Christology; but his use of the word " benefits " is significant.

with the living Christ but the assurance "that he had taken away *my* sins, even *mine*, and saved me from the law of sin and death." It is evident also in the familiar words of the Westminster Shorter Catechism, which, after expounding the historical work of Christ, asks the question, "How are we made partakers of the redemption purchased by Christ?" and gives the answer, "We are made partakers of the redemption purchased by Christ by the effectual application of it to us by his Holy Spirit."[8] The decisive factor is something which can be spoken of as "it."

The merit of this conception is obvious. The gospel is here firmly anchored to the historical facts of the incarnate life of Christ, and it can, therefore, be objectively established and protected against corruption into an instrument of ecclesiastical pretension or dissolution into a vague and indeterminate mysticism. The demerit of the conception is equally obvious: it tends to construe the religious relationship in impersonal terms. When Luther spoke of justification by faith, he meant faith in Christ; but to many of his successors it came to mean faith in justification. It is significant that in the theology of Lutheran orthodoxy the personal relation to Christ, the "mystical union," was isolated and set at a distance from justification in the plan of salvation (*ordo salutis*). The same tendency is apparent in the Reformed branch of Protestantism, where faith often came to mean faith in the Bible. In both, faith was a doctrinaire, propositional affair rather than a living personal relationship; and the piety, which was regulated by this faith, tended to become a cold, hard, formal thing. It is no wonder, therefore, that a recurring feature of Protestant history has been what we may call the revolt of piety against faith; for piety cannot thrive in the context of an impersonal and propositional faith; it seeks attachment to the person of Christ. The eighteenth century was marked by a series of such revolts throughout the Protestant world. German pietism was a revolt

[8] Q. 29.

against Lutheran orthodoxy and Reformed Biblicism; English Methodism, which was its offshoot, was a revolt against Anglican formalism; the opposition of "Evangelicals" and "Moderates" in Scotland and the Great Awakening in America are further examples of the struggle of piety to escape the deadening influence of a faith that is attached to an impersonal object. The revolt continued sporadically throughout the nineteenth century; and it flared up in the vogue of a Christian mysticism, which was the special object of Herrmann's attack.

This tension between piety and orthodoxy within Protestantism well illustrates the manner in which Christian disunity can arise from partiality of perspectives. Piety and orthodoxy each represents a valid perspective on the gospel. In other words, each of them concentrates upon a genuine part or aspect of the whole fact of Christ. It is only because each is relatively blind to what the other sees that tension arises between them. The Christ of Protestant orthodoxy is the Christ of Calvary, the Christ whose decisive deed for the salvation of the world was wrought once for all on the cross. The Christ with whom piety seeks personal communion is the Christ of Easter, the everliving Lord who has promised to be with us always. They are, of course, one and the same Christ. Both sides know this. Orthodoxy has never sought to deny that the Christ of Calvary is also the living Lord, nor piety that the living Lord is also the Christ who died. Yet the recurrent tension between them shows that though each is capable of verbally affirming the other's position, it is not really able to integrate it with its own. And thus, in effect, Christ is divided, the Christ of Calvary against the Christ of Easter.

The fragmentation of the gospel is apparent also in the great antithesis of "catholic" and "protestant." The Amsterdam Assembly of the World Council of Churches found here "our deepest difference" in regard to current views of the church. According to the Report of Section I, the difference is that "the emphasis usually called 'catholic' contains a primary insistence upon the visible continuity of the church in the apostolic succession of the episcopate," whereas "the one usually called 'protestant' primarily emphasizes the initiative of the Word of God and the response of faith, focused in the doctrine of justification *sola fide*."[9] W. M. Horton has pointed out that these two emphases reflect two views of the relation between the church and Christ; the catholic view he describes as "horizontal" and essentially *backward-looking*, the protestant as "vertical" and *upward-looking*.[10] These descriptions, however, although plausible in their way, are oversimplifications, which exaggerate the difference between the two views. The real situation is more complex; and there are some respects in which Dr. Horton's characterizations might be interchanged. Catholicism does, indeed, look back to Christ; it constantly appeals to the historical facts of the incarnate life. But it does this, not because it seeks the norm of its faith in the historical facts, but in order to authenticate its own claims to be the legitimate successor and plenipotentiary of Christ. The complaint of the Protestant Reformation against Catholicism was precisely that it did not look back, it did not submit itself to the judgment of the historical facts, but adjusted the historical facts to its own understanding of itself. By the same token, although it seems plausible to represent continuity with the Word made flesh as a distinctively catholic concern and the "actuality" of the Word in the present life of the church as distinctively protestant, a closer view reveals not only that both concerns are shared by both sides, but that even the difference of emphasis between them is contrary to the popular conception. The actuality of the gospel is the basic concern of both catholicism and protestantism. Both ask the question, how that which was accomplished by Christ in the historical work of his incarnate life can be transmitted, conveyed, actualized in the present and communicated to men today. The catholic

[9] *Amsterdam Assembly Series I,* p. 205. Harper & Brothers, 1948.
[10] *Ecumenical Review, I,* p. 374.

answer is the appeal to continuity. By this is meant that the communication of the gospel is effectively guaranteed by the continuity of the church with Christ; for by this continuity the church is held to be established as the legitimate successor of Christ, which has inherited from him the authority and the power to repeat his work. The focus of attention in catholicism is not the historical fact of Christ, but the alleged "extension of the incarnation" in the church. As Regin Prenter has said: "The incarnation of the saving God is continued in the tradition of the church in worship and doctrine, concentrated in the ministry of the church. In catholicism the church is above all the visible institution of salvation."[11] In the Mass the sacrifice of Christ on Calvary is daily repeated in bloodless form, and thereby the benefits of his passion are made present and actual to the contemporary Christian. *Backward-looking* is precisely what catholicism is not; catholicism has no need to refer back to the facts of history, for they are present reality in what the church does; and the validity of what the church does is guaranteed by what the church is. When the appeal is made to history in catholicism, it is not for the sake of authenticating the gospel, but for the sake of validating the claim of the church to be the authorized custodian and dispenser of the gospel. The claim is based on the dominical institution of the church in Matt. 16:18, together with the theory of the apostolic succession and the gift of the Holy Spirit, which is understood as a supernatural endowment to enable the church to perform its divinely appointed office.

The objection of the Protestant Reformation to this position was that it equates the original gospel with the ecclesiastical reproduction of it, and that it contains no effective safeguard against the risk that the reproduction may become an unrecognizable travesty of the original. The Reformers recognized the necessity of the reproduction of the gospel; but they were concerned with its authenticity, i.e., with the identity of the repro-

[11] *Ecumenical Review, I,* p. 383.

duction with the original. They held that this could not be guaranteed by the historical continuity of the church with Christ (even if that could be established), but only by constant critical recurrence to the original, as it had been preserved in the apostolic testimony. Thus *backward-looking* is a description that could more aptly be applied to Protestantism. Protestantism looks back to the Scriptures, because it accords to the original gospel, as it is attested there, a normative authority over all reproduction, repetition, or representation. It does not deny the importance of the latter, which underlies the catholic concern with continuity. But it sees in the catholic identification of continuity with succession or replacement a danger to the evangelical character of the gospel, which is bound up with the sufficiency, the finality, the once-for-all-ness of the work of Christ. A gospel that is directly continued in the offices of the church tends to lose its evangelical character; like a serial story, which is continued through successive issues of a magazine, it holds us in suspense, because we are uncertain how it will end. The gospel is the gospel because it is finished and complete; *tetelestai* (John 19:30). It does not need to be continued or repeated; for it is done, once for all; it needs only to be presented in its completeness to the contemporary believer. And here protestantism looks, not to the power of the church, but to the promise of the Spirit, whose office it is to take the things of Christ and show them to us.

For both catholicism and protestantism the gospel is like an ellipse, which has two foci, the historical work of the incarnate Christ and the reproduction or representation of it in the continuing work of the church. For both of them the former is associated with the cross and the latter with the gift of the Spirit. For both of them the gospel comprises Calvary and Pentecost. The difference between them is a difference of emphasis on these two foci, the catholic emphasizing the reproduction of the gospel in the church with the aid of the Holy Spirit, and the protestant emphasizing the finality of the work of the incarnate Christ. Under stress of controversy this difference of emphasis or perspective has often been magnified into a difference of view. Catholicism has become so preoccupied with the continuing power of the church that it has become relatively indifferent to the historical work of Christ. Bishop Newbigin gives an excellent illustration of this in his account of a meeting at which he was present and at which a Protestant and a Roman Catholic read papers on the Christian doctrine of forgiveness. "The Protestant paper dealt mainly with the meaning of the atonement. The Roman Catholic, in a forty-minute paper, did not once mention the death of Christ. Beginning from the word of Christ to Peter he explained that the authority to forgive sins which had then been conferred had been transmitted in uninterrupted succession through the centuries and was now possessed by the church to be dispensed to men. The church thus meets men in this respect not as Christ's representative, but as Christ, possessing in *itself* without reference to any higher source, the power to forgive sins. The church replaces Christ, and it becomes no longer necessary to refer to the event by which the church was initially called into being."[12] In protestantism, on the other hand, preoccupation with the historical work of Christ has led to a relative indifference to the doctrines of the Spirit and the church, especially in the Reformed tradition, in which, despite the prominence given them by Calvin, they practically passed from serious consideration, until they were

[12] Newbigin, *The Reunion of the Church,* p. 61. S. C. M. Press Ltd., 1948. This is also what Luther meant when he accused his two great opponents, the pope and the "Enthusiasts," of the same fundamental error of claiming that possession of the Spirit set them above the Word: "Likewise the papacy is sheer Enthusiasm, whereby the pope boasts that he has all laws in the shrine of his heart, so that whatever he decides and commands in his church is spirit and right, even though it goes beyond and against Scripture and the spoken Word" (*Articles of Schmalkald, WA,* 50, 245). The doctrine of the *magisterium,* climaxed in the dogma of papal infallibility, is the most perfect example of the, supposedly protestant, "principle of private judgment."

brought to attention by the ecumenical movement in the present century.[13] Protestant theology has been above all else a theology of the cross, and it has rarely recognized the problem of the transmission or communication of the gospel.

The fragmentation of the gospel is also apparent in the division between the Eastern and Western churches, and here it presents its deepest aspect. There is, as we have seen, a basic identity of view between catholicism and protestantism; both share a common perspective on the gospel, though with a considerable variation of emphasis within the area of agreement. This is because they both belong to the Western tradition of Christendom; both stand in the succession of Augustine, who put its distinctive stamp upon Western Christianity. Eastern Christianity is different from both; it employs a different norm; it looks at the gospel from a different perspective.

The theology of the Eastern church, as is well known, is characterized by a dominant interest in the incarnation; it is primarily an incarnational theology. To employ the scheme we have adopted, we may say that its attention is focused, not on Pentecost, as in catholicism, nor on Calvary, as in protestantism, but rather on Bethlehem, where the Word was made flesh. Christology, the problem of the person of Christ and the meaning of his assumption of our nature, is the theme that ever increasingly engrossed the minds of the fathers of the ancient church – not, indeed, to the exclusion of all thought of the work of Christ or of the Holy Spirit; but the profundity and subtlety of the thought they devoted to Christology, contrasted with their ingenuous and sometimes crude conceptions of the atonement, and their fragmentary and inadequate treatment of the Holy Spirit, shows clearly how their interest was distributed.

The interest of Eastern theology in the incarnation corre-

13 It is significant that there is no chapter on the Holy Spirit in the Westminster Confession (original form), and no question on the church in the Shorter Catechism.

sponds to a specific view of the human predicament. In the early Eastern church man's need of salvation is seen, not so much in his sin, as rather in the corruption incidental to sin. This corruption pertains to man's nature, and it is manifest above all in his liability to death.

The contrast with the West is, of course, not absolute. Although the Western church has been concerned chiefly with sin as a matter of the will by which man incurs guilt, it has always known that sin brings consequences in its train. Augustine, who did more than any other to shape the mind of the Western church in this matter, knew well the disabling effects of sin on man's nature; and those who are familiar with the Shorter Catechism will recall the vigorous terms in which it describes "the misery of that estate whereinto man fell."[14] But the Western church has always held that the gospel avails primarily to remove the guilt of sin and it has been relatively unconcerned with its application to the consequences of sin. In like manner the fathers of the Eastern church knew that the corruption of nature with which they were concerned was rooted in sin, but they looked to the gospel for a comprehensive salvation of the whole man by the restitution of his corrupted nature and not merely the forgiveness of his guilt. It is this concern which underlies the preoccupation of the ancient church with the doctrine of the incarnation or "Christology" in the traditional sense of the term; the incarnation, the assumption of our nature by the eternal Word, was to them the means of effecting a transmutation or "transubstantiation" of the corrupted nature of man. Their interest in the Christological problem was not psychological – except in a very minor degree; it was soteriological. They were not greatly concerned with solving the psychological problem of how divinity and humanity can be united in one person; what made the union of full divinity and full humanity in the one person of Christ important to them was the conviction that only one who was

[14] Answer to Q. 19.

" of one substance with the Father as regards his Godhead " could possess the divine properties of incorruptibility (*aphtharsia*) and immortality (*athanasia*), and only one who was " at the same time of one substance with us as regards his manhood " could impart them to us. The Definition of Chalcedon has nothing to say about the historical work of the incarnate Christ; it is entirely concerned with the terms of the hypostatic union, because this was regarded as the decisive factor in the gospel. By uniting our human nature with his divine nature Christ has (in principle at least) transformed its substance.

The view that the decisive relation between Christ and those he came to save is established at the level of nature explains the relative unconcern of the ancient church with the historical work of the incarnate Christ and with the problem of the communication of the gospel to those who are not contemporaneous with the incarnation. We search in vain in the writings of the fathers for any considered treatment of the question, " How are we made partakers of the redemption purchased by Christ? "[15] The question simply did not exist for them, because, they held, we are already partakers of Christ by virtue of his assumption of our nature, which established an ontological relation between us and him. By the same token it was relatively unimportant to define what Christ wrought in our nature; for the decisive thing in our salvation was not so much the precise character of his work as rather that community of nature between us and him, in virtue of which his work accrues to us. The definition of the person of Christ was the *articulus stantis et cadentis ecclesiae*.

These three areas of tension or dissension have been cited as examples of the fragmentation of the gospel, manifested

[15] *Shorter Catechism*, Q. 29. Compare the lame conclusion of Athanasius' *On the Incarnation*.

in partiality of perspectives upon the total fact of Christ. The tendency from the beginning has been to concentrate attention on one part or aspect of the fact of Christ, to lay a disproportionate emphasis on it, and, by implication, to pit it against the others. The tension within evangelical Protestantism between orthodox faith, which lays the emphasis on the historical work of Christ, and piety, which seeks personal communion with the living Christ, reflects a tendency to divorce the Christ of Calvary from the Christ of Easter. The antithesis between catholicism, which lays the emphasis on the actuality of the gospel in the continuing life of the church, and protestantism, which stresses the finality and sufficiency of the historical work of Christ, points to a similar division between Pentecost and Calvary. And the incarnational theology of the Eastern church represents a concentration on the Christ of Bethlehem, to the relative neglect of both Calvary and Pentecost. Nowhere, of course, are the neglected elements denied or ignored completely. In every case it is a matter of emphasis or perspective; one element is set in the foreground and magnified out of proportion, with the result that, not only is the total picture distorted, but that one element, not being viewed in proper relation to its context, becomes increasingly dependent for its significance on considerations derived from extraneous sources. A notable feature of the fragmentation of the gospel, which we have traced, is the development of theories around the various perspectives. The incarnational theology of the ancient church involved a metaphysical theory about human nature. The catholic emphasis on the continuation of the gospel in the church has involved theories of ecclesiastical power, apostolic succession, and papal infallibility. And the protestant preoccupation with the cross has caused a veritable flood of theories of the atonement. Often it is these theories which present the most obstinate barriers to mutual understanding. It may not be possible to get rid of theories altogether in the theological interpretation of the gospel. But this proliferation

of theories does seem to point to a failure to view the gospel as a whole and a tendency to seek the answers to the questions raised by its constituent parts anywhere but in the place where they are most likely to be found, viz., the contextual parts of the gospel itself.

The fragmentation of the gospel was begun through the preoccupation of the Greek fathers with Christology. When attention was turned to the atonement in the Latin West, there was an opportunity to recover something of the wholeness of the gospel, and perhaps this was part of the intention of Anselm, who inaugurated the Western debate on the atonement; for in calling his treatise "Why the God-man?" rather than "Why did the God-man die?" he pointed to the Christological question, and he skillfully attempted to integrate the Chalcedonian Christology in his interpretation of the atonement. But as the debate continued, interest came to be increasingly concentrated on the atonement, to the relative neglect of the incarnation, and the consequence was the development of theories of the atonement that are barely compatible with the doctrine of the incarnation. The type of theory that gained the widest currency in the Western church, and that saw the death of Christ as an act directed toward God in order to procure forgiveness from him, tended, in the words of Aulén, to "obscure the fact that the work of reconciliation and redemption is altogether the work of divine love." [16] The tendency was deplored by the writer of the essay on the atonement, in *Lux Mundi*, nearly seventy years ago, and he ascribed it, rightly, to the false isolation of this doctrine from its context: "In the course of religious controversy this doctrine has become separated from the rest, at one time neglected, at another overemphasized, till in its isolation it has been so stated as to be almost incredible." [17] It was revulsion against

[16] Aulén, *The Faith of the Christian Church,* p. 220. Muhlenberg Press, 1948.

[17] Arthur Lyttelton, in *Lux Mundi,* p. 229. (New York, 1889.) The doctrine of the atonement is reviewed in Ch. 7 of the present work.

the current interpretation of the doctrine of the atonement, as Bishop K. E. Kirk pointed out, that brought about the marked shift of interest from the atonement to the incarnation in the Church of England; and he remarks of Gore, whom he describes as "at once the victim and the prophet of this tendency," that in his Bampton Lectures, which he devoted to the subject of the incarnation, he cast only a cursory glance at the atonement.[18]

But the revival of interest in the incarnation, which, although it has been specially marked in Anglican theology, has spread beyond its confines, has often isolated this doctrine in a way that gets it out of focus. In many cases the unique event has been dissolved into a general principle; and then, as Niebuhr puts it, "the incarnation is regarded, not so much as the bearer of the revelation of divine mercy, as the assurance that the gulf between the finite and the eternal, between man and God, between history and superhistory, is not unbridgeable."[19] A notable exponent of this type of incarnational theology was Phillips Brooks. "God and man," he declared, "are essentially so near together that the meeting of their natures in the life of a God-man is not strange. . . . God *did* become man, and therefore manhood must be essentially capacious of divinity. . . . The great truth of the incarnation is that a perfectly pure obedient humanity might utter divinity, might be the transparent medium through which even God might show himself." This theme is said by the writer of the article, from which these quotations are derived, to have been the hub about which his preaching turned.[20] It may also have contributed to the remarkable power of its appeal. The conception was congenial to the temper of the latter half of the

[18] K. E. Kirk, *The Coherence of Christian Doctrine,* p. 5. S. P. C. K., London, 1950.

[19] Reinhold Niebuhr, *Nature and Destiny of Man, I,* p. 154. Charles Scribner's Sons, 1941.

[20] "Phillips Brooks and the Incarnation," Francis G. Ensley, in *Religion in Life,* Vol. XX, pp. 350–361. 1951.

nineteenth century, and there is still a considerable body of theological opinion, in America at all events, which is partial toward it. The writer of the article on Phillips Brooks maintains that his idea of the incarnation as a universal law, "of which the Life in Galilee is the one supreme illustration," is the true alternative to what he terms the "inherently unpreachable theology" of orthodoxy, old and new. As late as 1913 Pringle-Pattison declared in his Gifford Lectures at Aberdeen: "Few things are more disheartening to the philosophical student of religion than the way in which the implications of the doctrine of the incarnation are evaded in popular theology by dividing the functions of Deity between the Father and the Son, conceived practically as two distinct personalities, or centers of consciousness, the Father perpetuating the old monarchical ideal and the incarnation of the Son being limited to a single historical individual."[21] It is clear that this philosophical apology for the doctrine of the incarnation, which derives from Hegel, and which seeks to make it acceptable to man by presenting it as the truth about himself, not only isolates it from, but opposes it to, the doctrine of the atonement; for the truth that it is made to yield is very different from that which is exposed in the doctrine of the atonement.

Happily there are evidences in contemporary theological thought of a turning away from these arbitrary and eclectic emphases, which inevitably distort the picture of the gospel, and an awareness of the importance of recovering what Leonard Hodgson has called "the organic wholeness of the Christian faith."[22] In a lecture given shortly before his death the late Bishop of Oxford argued that if "neither the doctrine of the atonement nor that of the incarnation is held today with that fullness of conviction and understanding which once it

[21] A. S. Pringle-Pattison, *The Idea of God*, p. 409. Oxford University Press, 1920.

[22] Leonard Hodgson, in *Essays on the Trinity and the Incarnation*, p. 363. Longmans, 1928.

commanded," the reason is the false exaltation of the one against the other as the fundamental Christian truth, and he pleaded for coherent thinking about them: "Only as they are brought together once more in their fullness will either of them become intelligible, and the two together have converting power."[23]

The reintegration of incarnation and atonement is the task that is attempted in the present work. But the thesis is that this task cannot be accomplished unless it is seen as part of a task that is even more comprehensive in its scope. It will be maintained that the severance between incarnation and atonement is the result of a failure to grasp the link that connects them, viz., the historical life of the incarnate Christ which is attested in the Evangelical records, or, in other words, that if one party has sought to find the essence of the gospel at Bethlehem, and another at Calvary, and each of them thereby presented a distorted picture of the gospel, it is because neither of them took sufficient account of what lay between, in Galilee and Judea. It is at this point that the task of theological integration will be taken up.

[23] Kirk, *op. cit.*, p. 5.

CHAPTER

II

The Jesus of History

It is generally agreed that the most important event in Protestant theology during the last hundred years was the "rediscovery of the Jesus of history." The significance of the Jesus-of-history movement and the effects of its impact upon theological thought have been so well discussed by the late D. M. Baillie in his admirable book *God Was in Christ* that it would be superfluous to attempt to cover the same ground. But two or three comments and observations may be added by way of relating it to our present inquiry.

The immediate effect of the rediscovery of the Jesus of history was to introduce a tension into Protestant thinking, which reached its height in the early years of the present century. The debates about the Jesus of history and the Christ of faith, which were set off by Harnack's *What Is Christianity?* reflected a widespread feeling that a radically new perspective on the gospel had been opened up which presented a serious challenge to traditional orthodoxy. In the language we have used we may say that the Christ of Galilee was now pitted against the Christ of Bethlehem and Calvary and Easter and Pentecost, and, it may be added, of Nicaea and Chalcedon. The effect was the emergence of a new "norm," as the title of Harnack's book indicates – a norm that involved a rereading, a reinterpretation of the essence of Christianity: the "simple Galilean gospel," presented as the message of the Fatherhood of God, the brotherhood of man, the value of the individual and other similar formulations, was put forward in opposition to the traditional gospel of salvation, which, it was alleged, had been superimposed upon it by others, especially Paul, who sometimes figured as the villain in the case. This simplification of the gospel gave the movement a considerable appeal, which was increased by two other factors. It went a long way toward meeting the need for a personal object of devotion: the Jesus of history became a living person for many people who had been unable to feel any kind of personal relation to the Christ of the orthodox creeds. And it redirected attention to the teaching of Jesus, which, it was commonly felt, "had been lost to sight behind a defensive screen of metaphysics gathered round it by the church."[1]

The Jesus-of-history movement is now a spent force. Three things helped to check its impetus. (1) The first was the increasing realization that the attempted simplification of the gospel was a gross oversimplification. It was impossible to set up an antithesis between the Jesus of history and the Christ of faith, because it is impossible to take the Jesus of history seriously without being led to the questions of traditional Christology. As Baillie put it, "The Jesus of history himself can tell us that the Jesus of history is not enough."[2] (2) The second was the rise of form criticism, which questioned the assumption that a portrait of the historical Jesus could be recovered from the Gospel records, since those records had been shaped by the needs of the kerygma of the primitive church, and "the telling of the story of Jesus was Christological through and through from the start."[3] (3) The third was the rise of the neo-orthodox theology, which reasserted the orthodox perspective upon the gospel in a challenging way.

It has become impossible to pit the Jesus of history against the Christ of faith in the way some tried to do in the early

[1] H. R. Mackintosh, *Types of Modern Theology*, p. 15. James Nisbet, & Co., Ltd., London, 1937.

[2] D. M. Baillie, *God Was in Christ*, p. 42. Faber and Faber, London, 1948.

[3] *Op. cit.*, p. 60.

years of this century; but this does not mean that the whole movement can be dismissed as a *faux pas.* The rediscovery of the Jesus of history may not have meant what it was thought to mean, but it does have a meaning; it may not present a new norm in opposition to that of traditional orthodoxy, but it does point to an element of which it is doubtful whether traditional orthodoxy takes sufficient account, viz., the historical life of the incarnate Lord. The question is not disposed of by pointing, with the form critics, to the difficulty of recovering the portrait of the historical Jesus; the fact remains that there was a historical life and that it was considered an essential part of the record, and the question is: whether and how it can be integrated with the traditional pattern of orthodoxy.

The question is presented in a provocative way by neo-orthodoxy, which has tended to disparage the historical aspect of the fact of Christ as of little or no consequence in the faith, which centers on the risen and exalted Lord. Baillie expressed a general feeling when in a well-known passage of his book he brought the charge against the theology of Karl Barth that it has no real attachment to the Jesus of history: " His theology has become so austerely a theology of the Word, that it is hardly a theology of the Word-made-Flesh." [4] And on this account, Baillie felt, " It does not take the incarnation quite seriously." [5] In particular, it is felt by many that the teaching of Jesus receives very inadequate attention in neo-orthodoxy. H. R. Mackintosh gave it as his opinion that " Barth's theology has still to adjust itself to the teaching of Jesus," [6] and Baillie clearly points to the same thing when he quotes Weinel's assertion that it was the content of the teaching of Jesus, especially his teaching about human sin and divine forgiveness,

[4] *Op. cit.*, p. 53.

[5] *Op. cit.*, p. 47.

[6] From a private letter, written in 1933, just after he had given the lecture on Barth which appears in *Types of Modern Theology*. The passage continued " not, of course, to everything in the teaching of Jesus, but to much in it that is important."

more than any Christology, that distinguished Christianity, and he adds: "That may well seem to some to be a salutary reminder today, in face of those schools of theological thought which make a great deal of Christology, but make very little of our Lord's own teaching, though he spent so much time upon it in the days of his flesh." [7]

It would, however, be a mistake to suppose that the problem arises only in connection with the theology of Karl Barth. Although the rediscovery of the Jesus of history has raised it in an acute way in contemporary theology, the problem of finding an integral place for the human life of the incarnate Lord within the framework of orthodoxy has haunted Protestant theology from the beginning. Calvin was aware of it, and it is instructive to observe how he tried to deal with it. Calvin noted the omission of any reference to the historical life of Christ in the Apostles' Creed; he refers to the matter more than once and was evidently much exercised by it. In the *Geneva Catechism* (1542) he poses this question about the Creed: "*Pourquoi de la nativité viens tu incontinent à la mort, laissant toute l'histoire de sa vie?*" and he gives the answer: "*Pour ce qu'il n'est ici parlé que de ce qui est proprement de la substance de nostre redemption.*" [8] It is evident, however, that this dismissal of "the whole story of his life" as not belonging to "the substance of our redemption" was too cavalier to satisfy the mind of Calvin, and we find him groping after a more satisfactory explanation. Twice in the *Institutes* he returns to this question of the "incontinence" of the Creed, and he suggests two answers. One is that the whole history of Christ's life was implicitly subsumed under the "suffered" of the Creed: "It may be truly said, not only that he was perpetually burdened with a cross during his sojourn on earth, but that his whole life was nothing but a kind of perpetual cross." [9] In

[7] Baillie, *op. cit.*, p. 61.

[8] Q. 55 (*Bekenntnisschriften der reformierten Kirche,* ed. by Niesel, p. 8).

[9] *Inst.*, III, 8. 1.

the other passage Calvin suggests that the common denominator of Christ's life and death is to be found in his obedience. If it be asked, he says, how Christ made atonement for our sins, "the general answer is that he did it by the whole course of his obedience." So, while it is true that "Scripture ascribes this in a peculiar manner to the death of Christ," and "therefore, in the so-called Apostles' Creed there is very properly an immediate transition from the birth of Christ to his death and resurrection, in which the sum of perfect salvation consists, yet there is no exclusion of the rest of the obedience which he performed in his life." [10]

The special problem of according a significant place to the teaching of Jesus was also present to the mind of Calvin – it could hardly escape the notice of one who devoted himself so much to the exposition of Scripture. It had been customary in theological treatment of the work of Christ to schematize it as the twofold office (*munus duplex*) of priest and king, the priestly office (*munus sacerdotale*) being related to his sacrificial death, and the kingly (*munus regium*) to his resurrection and exaltation. Calvin himself appears to have been content with this scheme at the outset, but later he made a practice of adding the prophetic office of Christ, and changed (or restored) the *munus duplex* to *munus triplex*. The change appeared for the first time in the *Geneva Catechism* of 1542 and thereafter in the *Institutes*.[11] The *munus triplex* subsequently became a commonplace of both Reformed and Lutheran theologies.

The inclusion of the prophetic among the offices of Christ marks a clear recognition on the part of Calvin that the teaching is an important element in the history of Christ and that it cannot be "incontinently" passed over in a theological account of his life and work. At the same time the manner in which

[10] *Inst.*, II, 16. 5.

[11] *Cat. Genev.*, Q. 44: *Inst.*, II, 15. There is some question whether Calvin originated or merely rehabilitated the doctrine of the *munus triplex*, but this does not affect the point.

Calvin includes it as one element in a threefold office attests his firm belief that it is capable of being integrated in the traditional view of the gospel. Calvin, of course, adheres to the characteristic Western norm; his picture of the gospel is dominated by Calvary and Easter; but he saw that Galilee must also have a place in it, and he thought it could have a place in it without destroying the pattern of the picture as a whole.

These are indications that Calvin was aware of the problem. He cannot, however, be said to have solved it. The formulas he used, obedience and suffering, are partially successful in integrating the historical life of Jesus with the main theme of the gospel, but they do not give it a really essential place. The fundamental structure of the gospel would remain intact, even if Calvin were to pass " incontinently " from the Nativity to the Passion and omit the whole story of his life. And this is true of Western theology generally. Where the perspective is upon the Christ of Calvary, the Christ of Galilee tends to be reduced to relative insignificance. It is no accident that the problem has arisen again in contemporary theology, in which there is a powerful trend toward reaffirmation of the traditional Western norm. As we have already noted, neo-orthodoxy is felt by some critics to display a marked lack of interest in the historical life of Jesus,[12] and is even suspected of regarding it as expendable. The fact of the historical life is emphasized; the actual content of it is not.

While the problem has been reopened in our time with the revival of orthodoxy supervening upon the revival of interest in the Jesus of history, it has been intensified by an influential trend in New Testament study, which would base the Western theological norm in the primitive apostolic preaching. The work of C. H. Dodd [13] may be regarded in a sense as a vindication of the Protestant principle by the demonstration that

[12] Baillie, *op. cit.*, pp. 34 ff.

[13] C. H. Dodd, *The Apostolic Preaching and Its Developments*, 2d edit., Hodder & Stoughton, 1944.

the norm of orthodoxy has the authority of Scripture; in effect, it confirms the suspicion that the Scriptural principle of Protestantism had a distinct bias from the outset. The formal principle of the authority of Scripture was itself regulated by the material principle of justification by faith, and *sola Scriptura* meant in actual practice *sola Paulina Scriptura.* Luther, as is well known, made no secret of it. But the question is whether such eclecticism (acknowledged or not) is really compatible with the authority of Scripture, whether it is not equivalent to the establishment of a canon within the canon.

It is the same question that is carried back to the New Testament itself by Dodd. The main facts that emerge from his studies of the primitive kerygma may be summarized as follows:

1. The death of Christ, together with his resurrection, occupied the central place in the apostolic presentation of the gospel from the beginning. According to Paul, the death of Christ formed the basic element of the tradition which he had received and which he was commissioned to proclaim. "For I delivered unto you first of all that which I also received, how that Christ died for our sins" (I Cor. 15:3). For him the gospel was concentrated in "Jesus Christ, and him crucified" (I Cor. 2:2). The same emphasis appears in the accounts of the early preaching in the book of The Acts.[14] The work of Christ was pre-eminently the work of his death.

2. The death of Christ, although given the central place, was not presented in complete isolation. It usually appears in the company of a number of other elements, especially the fulfillment of prophecy, the Davidic sonship, and the expected consummation. Some variation in the selection and arrangement of these elements may be observed, especially between Paul and "the Jerusalem Kerygma of Acts,"[15] but by and large they may be said to have formed the indispensable context of the death of Christ, apart from which it could not be significantly presented.

[14] Dodd, *op. cit.*, pp. 21 f.

[15] Dodd, *op. cit.*, p. 25.

3. The third and (to us at least) the most striking fact is the absence from the Pauline kerygma of any explicit reference to the ministry of Jesus in his incarnate life. Peter in his speeches makes reference to the miracles (Acts 2:22), the teaching (Acts 3:22), and in one passage (Acts 10:34–43) he gives what may be called "an outline of the life of Jesus," but of all this there is scarcely a trace in the kerygma of Paul. Was Paul indifferent to the incarnate life of Jesus? That he was ignorant of it is a possibility that may confidently be discounted. Why then was he all but completely silent about it?

The question has been much discussed, and various answers have been suggested. It may be that in his actual preaching Paul had more to say about the life and ministry of Jesus than the evidence of his epistles leads us to suppose. Dodd points to the account in Acts 13:16–41 of the speech delivered by Paul at Pisidian Antioch, which contains a number of specific allusions to episodes in the Gospel story, and he argues that "if we recall the close general similarity of the kerygma as derived from Acts, as well as Paul's emphatic assertion of the identity of his gospel with the general Christian tradition, we shall not find it altogether incredible that the speech at Pisidian Antioch may represent in a general way one form of Paul's preaching, that form, perhaps, which he adopted in synagogues when he had the opportunity of speaking there. If that is so, then we must say that he, like other early Christian preachers, gave a place in his preaching to some kind of recital of the facts of the life and ministry of Jesus."[16] That may be so. Still, the absence of such recitals from the epistles remains puzzling. H. A. A. Kennedy offered the explanation that there was no occasion for them there; recalling that the epistles were not missionary addresses but in every instance written to men and women who were already believers in Christ and who had received at least some training within the Christian community, he argued, "It is surely obvious that he will take for granted a more or less accurate acquaintance on their part with

[16] Dodd, *op. cit.*, p. 30.

the salient features of Jesus' character and history."[17] The argument is plausible; but it is special pleading to invoke it only in this matter. If there is anything with which the people to whom Paul wrote may be presumed to have been familiar, it is the death of Christ; yet the epistles abound with references to the death of Christ. Paul was not averse to retreading familiar ground, if he thought it was important.[18] The absence of reference to the life of Jesus in his epistles, especially those passages in which he rehearses the main elements of his gospel, points to the conclusion that it was not important. The evidence makes it impossible to agree with those who declare it is "reckless,"[19] or "idle"[20] to say that Paul had no interest in the historical Jesus. The facts of the incarnation – that Christ came in our flesh, that he was born of a woman and found in fashion as a man – are certainly essential elements in Paul's gospel; but the details of the incarnate life appear to have no place in it. Calvin's comment on the Apostles' Creed might also be applied to him: he skips incontinently from the birth to the death and omits the whole story of the life. The Pauline attitude comes very close to Kierkegaard, when he wrote, "If the contemporary generation had left behind them nothing but the words, 'We have believed that in such and such a year God appeared among us in the humble figure of a servant, that he lived and taught in our community; and finally died,' it would be more than enough."[21]

But it was less than enough for the early church, which, highly as it prized the writings of Paul, collected and recorded and eventually canonized a great deal of additional information about the history of Jesus. It is, of course, the presence of

[17] H. A. A. Kennedy, *The Theology of the Epistles*, p. 100. Gerald Duckworth & Co., Ltd., London, 1919.

[18] Eutychus could perhaps have confirmed this. Cf. Phil. 3:1.

[19] Kennedy, *op. cit.*, p. 100.

[20] Baillie, *op. cit.*, p. 45. Cf. Bultmann, *Theologie des Neuen Testaments*, p. 289. Mohr, Tübingen, 1948.

[21] Kierkegaard, *Philosophical Fragments*, p. 87. Princeton University Press, 1936.

the evangelical records in the canon of New Testament Scripture alongside the writings of Paul that raises the whole problem in the first place.

It would be very interesting to know what was in the mind of the church when it canonized the Synoptics and whether, in particular, it was aware of the variance of interest between them and the epistles. Dodd says that in much of the material incorporated in Matthew and Luke "we discern a certain departure from the original perspective and emphasis of the kerygma," [22] and he ascribes their adoption to a conscious act of self-correction or adaptation to changing circumstances on the part of the church: thus, as the fading of the eschatological hope obliged the church to readjust itself to the prospect of a continuing existence in the world, it became necessary to seek more guidance in its practical problems from the remembered teaching of Jesus (now recorded in Matthew); and as the church spread farther into territory where there was less understanding for Biblical and Jewish concepts, it became necessary to supplement the Marcan picture of the strong Son of God with the Matthean picture of the royal lawgiver and the Lucan picture of the friend and lover of men.[23] Whatever the reasons, the preservation of the Synoptic records reflects a belief that the history of Jesus possesses a greater significance than it had received in the primitive kerygma. The question is whether these additional emphases "represent sidetracks from the main line" of the apostolic preaching, as Dodd suggests,[24] or whether they represent attempts to supply elements that, though missing from the primitive kerygma, are integral to the very gospel it proclaimed.

[22] *Op. cit.*, p. 52. [23] *Op. cit.*, p. 54. [24] *Op. cit.*, p. 55.

CHAPTER

III

The Humanity of Christ in Eastern Theology

THE PROBLEM of the significance of the Jesus of history within the pattern of orthodoxy may be approached indirectly. We may ask whether theology discloses a lacuna, which may be connected in some way with the neglect of the historical Jesus: is there some theological aporia, some question to which theology has failed to find the answer, because, perhaps, it has failed to look for it in this quarter? This inquiry seems the more promising inasmuch as it involves comparative study of diverse theological traditions; since the neglect of the historical Jesus is common to all of them, more or less, it may be proper to inquire whether their variations can be traced to this single root, whether, in other words, their differences in norm and focus represent approaches from different standpoints to one fundamental problem.

A comparison between the Eastern and Western traditions will provide the essential clue. While Western theology, and Protestant theology in particular, has seen the focus of the gospel in the death of Christ, it has at the same time respected and sought to assimilate the insights of Eastern theology into the doctrine of the incarnation. The dogmatic definitions of the ancient church concerning the person of Christ have been assiduously cherished in the West, and they have been accepted for the most part as the standard of Christological orthodoxy. Yet the technical division of the doctrine of Christ into Christology and soteriology is an indication that the West has not been successful in integrating the classical doctrine of the person of Christ with its own distinctive interest in his work.

The reason is that in their passage from East to West the formulas of the classical Christology have undergone a sea change; they have lost one element of their original significance, which played an indispensable role in the soteriological thought of the ancient church, and the Western church has been compelled to try to fill up the resultant lacuna with material drawn from other sources.

It is true to say that the classical Christology declares Christ to be "true God" and "true man," but these simple phrases barely convey the full significance of the original formulas. Since God is one, true God can only mean one in being with God. To speak of Christ as God in any lesser sense than this – to say, for example, that Christ is a divine being, or an emissary from the divine – is to cut at the foundation of the faith. This is the point on which the church insisted at the Council of Nicaea, against the Arians; the council declared that there is only one sense in which we can affirm the "divinity" of Christ, and that is the Trinitarian sense – we must say he is *homo-ousios,* consubstantial, coessential, or one in being with the Father.

When the church declared that Christ is also "true man," it meant what the phrase means on the face of it – that Christ became a human being in the true sense of the word. Since human beings (unlike God) constitute a genus, it means that Christ became a member of the genus, a man like other men. Against views that Christ was less than truly human – that he lacked a human body or a human mind – the ancient church insisted that nothing that belongs to the definition of a complete human being was lacking in him. But the church went farther than this; it did not stop with the assertion that Christ was an authentic specimen of the genus "man" – indeed, its interest in making this assertion rests on a deeper ground, viz., on the view that in becoming man Christ entered into an ontological relation with the whole race of men. Had the church been concerned only to assert that Christ was a man like other men, his relation to man could have been expressed in the same term that the Semi-Arians used to express his relation to God – *homoi-ousios,* similar in being. But the Council of Chalcedon went farther than this: it defined Christ's relation to man in the same term in which the Council of Nicaea had defined his relation to God – "*homo-ousios* with the Father as to his Godhead, and the same *homo-ousios* with us as to his manhood." [1] By the use of this term the council clearly meant more than that Christ was a man like other men; it meant that, just as it was true to say that "God was in Christ," so also there is a sense in which it could be said that "man was in Christ."

With this affirmation of the *homo-ousia,* or consubstantiality, of Christ with men the council set the seal of orthodoxy upon a strain that had been present in patristic thought from the beginning. It is true that the fathers who have expressly formulated the idea are comparatively few in number; but since there is no evidence of any opposition to the idea in this period, it may be presumed that they were only making explicit what was implicit in the minds of their contemporaries. Moreover, since they include in their number some of the most eminent names in patristic thought, the presumption is that they alone were in command of the conceptual tools needed to express the idea. The idea is not an easy one to express, and it is far from clear what it meant even to those fathers who have given it fullest expression (the interpretation of their texts has never ceased to be controversial). But no one could so much as attempt to express it without a certain familiarity with the categories of Greek philosophical thought, and that could not be looked for then (or at any time) in more than an intellectual

[1] Cf. R. V. Sellers, *The Council of Chalcedon,* p. 210. S. P. C. K., London, 1953.

minority. This does not mean that the idea depends on the validity of the categories used to express it by this minority. On the contrary, it is probable that those categories were used because they seemed better adapted than any others previously devised to formulate an idea that was inherent in the faith from the beginning.

~

The idea, which is formulated in the Chalcedonian Definition as the consubstantiality of Christ with us as regards his manhood, is that of an ontological relation with mankind into which Christ entered by his incarnation and which forms the presupposition or precondition of his atoning work. The gospel, in its simplest terms, is the message of something done by Christ *for us*. To the ancient church it seemed — and rightly — that the vicarious character of the work of Christ could not rest solely upon our subjective appropriation of it (although, as we shall see, that was not excluded), but must have some prior, objective ground, and they sought this in the idea of an ontological relation between the incarnate Christ and human nature as a whole.

It was the more natural for them to think in this way because they came to the problem with a much deeper sense of the essential unity of mankind than we have today. It would probably be true to say that in the ancient world, both Hellenic and Hebraic, the unity or solidarity of mankind appeared as self-evident as the distinct individuality of individual men does to us, and therefore the problem of expressing the universal aspect of the incarnation was much less acute for them. If some of the fathers seem to have been satisfied with metaphysical concepts that are far from convincing to us, it is because there was no real problem for them here — or, at most, a problem of formulating a truth that was regarded as self-evident.

Of the fathers who expressed the idea prior to its incorporation in the Chalcedonian Definition, four may be cited: Athanasius, Gregory of Nyssa, Hilary of Poitiers, and Cyril of Alexandria.

Athanasius is often cited as the classical exponent of the idea, and this is true in the sense that it is he who develops its soteriological significance most fully. He has, however, less interest than some of his successors in spelling it out in philosophical terms. The idea is central to the thought of Athanasius, and many statements of it are to be found in his writings, especially his youthful masterpiece, *On the Incarnation of the Word,* and his later *Orations Against the Arians.* The following excerpt from the former would seem to contain all the essential points:

"For the Word, perceiving that not otherwise could the corruption of men be undone save by death as a necessary condition, while it was impossible for the Word to suffer death, being immortal, and Son of the Father; to this end he takes to himself a body capable of death, that it, by partaking of the Word who is above all, might be worthy to die in the stead of all, and might, because of the Word which was to come to dwell in it, remain incorruptible, and that thenceforth corruption might be stayed from all by the grace of the resurrection. Whence, by offering unto death the body he himself had taken, as an offering and sacrifice free from any stain, straightway he put away death from all his peers by the offering of an equivalent. For, being over all, the Word of God naturally by offering his own temple and corporeal instrument for the life of all satisfied the debt of his death. And thus he, the incorruptible Son of God, being conjoined with all by a like nature, naturally clothed all with incorruption, by the promise of the resurrection. For the actual corruption in death has no longer holding ground against men, by reason of the Word which by his one body has come to dwell among them." [2]

[2] Athanasius, *On the Incarnation,* c. 9 (LCC, III, p. 63). The Westminster Press, 1954.

Four points about the incarnation are made in this remarkably compact passage:

1. The assumption of a mortal body is the necessary condition of the experience of death by the incarnate Word.
2. The presence of the indwelling Word renders the death of the one body he assumed an equivalent for the death of all.
3. The presence of the indwelling Word, who is immortal and incorruptible, renders the body he assumed immune from corruption.
4. There is a relation between the incarnate Word and us, through which the incorruption achieved by him is communicated to us.

What is the relation? Athanasius speaks of it in two different ways. Sometimes he sees it in the Word or Logos himself as such: since the Logos who became incarnate is also the Logos by whom all things were made and of whom the human race in particular has been made to partake, there is a certain natural affinity between the Creator Logos and the logos which is in us; the latter is a reflection [3] or image [4] of the former. But more commonly he speaks of it in bodily terms: the relation between the body assumed by the Word and our bodies is such that the Word, by assuming one body, is present with all and dwells in all.[5] It never becomes clear, however, how this bodily relation is to be understood. It is significant, perhaps, that when he refers to it for the first time, Athanasius has recourse to an illustration – the famous illustration of the visiting monarch; it follows immediately on the passage quoted above:

"And like as when a great king has entered into some large city and taken up his abode in one of the houses there, such city is at all events held worthy of high honor, nor does any enemy or bandit any longer descend upon it and subject it;

[3] *On the Incarnation,* c. 3 (LCC, III, p. 58).
[4] *Against the Arians,* 2, 78.
[5] *On the Incarnation,* c. 9 (LCC, III, p. 63).

but, on the contrary, it is thought entitled to all care, because of the king's having taken up his residence in a single house there; so, too, has it been with the monarch of us all. For now that he has come to our realm, and taken up his abode in one body among his peers, henceforth the whole conspiracy of the enemy against mankind is checked, and the corruption of death which before was prevailing against them is done away. For the race of men had gone to ruin, had not the Lord and Savior of all, the Son of God, come among us to meet the end of death."[6]

Elsewhere Athanasius speaks of a similarity or kinship between his body and ours, but nowhere does he tell us precisely in what it consists, or how the benefit of the redemption accomplished by the incarnate Word comes to us through it. There can, however, be no doubt of the central importance of the idea in Athanasius' understanding of the Christian salvation; for he sometimes refers to it as if it were itself the decisive factor in the saving work of Christ, as if "by the mere bringing into physical contact in Christ of the divine and the human our salvation was effected,"[7] e.g., "Human nature and the divine are linked together in Christ, and thereby our salvation is established."[8]

In Gregory of Nyssa the conception is restated in more philosophical terms. The human nature that was assumed by the Son of God could only be taken from the lump of our humanity, since there was no human nature in heaven, and his incarnation, so to speak, leavens the whole lump: "Not from

[6] *Ibid.*

[7] Riviere, *The Doctrine of the Atonement: A Historical Study*, p. 174. Kegan Paul, London, 1909.

[8] *Against the Arians*, 2, 70. Riviere also cites *Against the Arians*, 2, 60: "Because the Word of God, the eternal Son of the Father, clothed himself with flesh and became man, we are delivered"; *Letter to Epictetus*, 7: "By the very fact that the Savior became man really and truly, the whole man was saved"; *Letter to Adelphius*, 6: "The Savior's presence in the flesh works our redemption and the salvation of every creature."

another source, but from the lump of our humanity, came the manhood which received the divine. By the resurrection it was exalted along with the Godhead. In the case of our own bodies the activity of one of our senses is felt throughout the whole system which is united to it. In just the same way, seeing that our nature contributes, as it were, a single living organism, the resurrection of one part of it extends to the whole. By the unity and continuity of our nature it is communicated from the part to the whole." [9] This unity of nature constitutes the medium in which the saving work, which Christ accomplished, is conveyed to us.

It has sometimes been thought that Gregory and the others of this school of thought conceived of salvation in a "physical" sense and that they supposed (or ought in consistency to have supposed) its communication from Christ to men to take place "mechanically" or "automatically." Some of the language used by the fathers would seem to lend support to these interpretations, as we have just seen in the case of Athanasius. But such language is usually found in summary references. Their more careful statements show that their real meaning was different.

When it is said that the Greek fathers conceived of salvation in a physical sense, this is not true if the word "physical" be taken in its modern sense, as the antithesis of spiritual; but it is true if the word be taken in its original, etymological sense of "belonging to man's nature" (*physis*). Man's nature is composite, and the Christian salvation applies to man's nature in its entirety, not merely to one element in it. Christ wrought salvation for the whole man, body and soul: "The manner of our salvation," says Gregory, "owes its efficacy less to instruction by teaching than to what he who entered into fellowship

[9] *Address on Religious Instruction* (*Catechetical Oration*) c. 32 (LCC, III, p. 310). Gregory's emphasis on the point that the humanity of the incarnate Logos was taken from the lump of our humanity is directed against the teaching of Apollinarius that the humanity was pre-existent in the mind of God. For the further significance of this, see note 40, p. 59.

with man actually did. In him life became a reality, so that by means of the flesh which he assumed and thereby deified salvation might come to all that was akin to it." [10]

Gregory also makes it clear that there was no thought of a mechanical or automatic communication of salvation from Christ to men. Despite his "physical" conception of the work that Christ did in our nature, its effect on our nature is only potential: "For when in the case of the man in whom he was incarnate the soul returned once more to the body after the dissolution, a similar union of the separated elements potentially [*te dynamei*] passed to the whole of human nature, as if a new beginning had been made." [11] For the potential to become actual something more is needed; the experience of the Master must be imitated or represented in the experience of the disciple, and this, according to Gregory, is the function of the sacraments, through which we are united with the human nature of Christ.[12] Yet, although there is a clear correspondence between the sacraments and the nature of the salvation which they mediate, Gregory guards against the thought that the sacraments convey salvation mechanically or *ex opere operato*. He is emphatic that without repentance and amendment of life all talk of baptismal regeneration is empty prattle.[13]

The idea of the consubstantiality of Christ with mankind is sometimes regarded as a peculiarity of the Greek fathers, but this is not quite correct. The Greek fathers were the first to formulate it, but the idea was also received in the Western church and it is found in several of the Latin fathers. Its most eminent, and, probably its earliest, expositor in the Western church was Hilary of Poitiers. Hilary may have acquired the idea from Greek sources; for he had spent some years in the East and he played an important part in mediating Greek

[10] *Op. cit.*, c. 35.
[11] *Op. cit.*, c. 16.
[12] *Op. cit.*, cc. 33–37.
[13] *Op. cit.*, c. 40.

thought to the West. But the manner in which he expounds it shows that it was readily assimilable by the Western mind.

Like Athanasius and Gregory, Hilary relates it basically to the incarnation. He sees the incarnation as establishing a relation between Christ and all mankind: "When the Word was made flesh and dwelt among us, that means he took to himself the nature of the entire human race."[14] More briefly, "he became our flesh universally."[15] Hilary does not discuss the question whether the universal, "flesh," or "human nature," is real; like Athanasius, he used an illustration; he compares the unity of Christ and mankind to a city (the "city set on a hill" of Matt. 5:14): "Just as a city consists of a varied multitude of inhabitants, so a certain union of the entire human race is contained in him by the nature of the body which he assumed. Thus, he is the city, in virtue of our being gathered together in him, and we form the population of the city through our association with his flesh" (*In Matt.* 4. c. 12). "He took to himself one flesh (or the flesh of one) that he might dwell inwardly in all flesh."[16]

Hilary's language sometimes gives the impression that he thinks of the incarnation as producing an effect on the whole human race "mechanically" or "automatically"; but this is not his real thought. The effect of the incarnation on the human race is, so to speak, potential; it becomes actual by the use of the sacraments – or perhaps it would be better to say that it is first objective and then subjective. Hilary's own way of expressing it is that by Christ's assumption of our flesh at the incarnation we are in him and by our partaking of the flesh of his body in the Eucharist, he is in us. This mutual indwelling is indivisible, and Hilary can say, "No one will be in Christ unless Christ be in him."[17] Nevertheless, he insists that the incarnation establishes a "natural" union between Christ and

[14] *Tract. in Ps.* 51, c. 17.
[15] *Tract. in Ps.* 54, c. 9 (*universitatis nostrae caro*).
[16] *De Trin.* 2, 25.
[17] *Ibid.*, 8, 16.

mankind, and he does this because he sees it as part of a complex but consistent pattern of union which originates in the union of Christ with the Father and culminates in our union with him: "He is in the Father by the nature of his divinity, we are in him by his corporal birth, and he is in us by the mystery of the Eucharist."[18] It is at every stage a natural union, or union of natures; to deny this at the incarnational or sacramental stages is, in the eyes of Hilary, to deny it also at the Christological:

"Now I ask those who bring forward a unity of will between Father and Son, whether Christ is in us today through verity of nature or through agreement of will. For if in truth the Word has been made flesh and we in very truth receive the Word made flesh as food from the Lord, are we not bound to believe that he abides in us naturally, who, born as a man, has assumed the nature of our flesh now inseparable from himself, and has conjoined the nature of his own flesh to the nature of the eternal Godhead in the sacrament by which his flesh is communicated to us? For so are we all one, because the Father is in Christ and Christ in us. Whosoever then shall deny that the Father is in Christ naturally must first deny that either he is himself in Christ naturally, or Christ in him, because the Father in Christ and Christ in us make us one in them."[19] For Hilary, the second *homo-ousios* of the Chalcedonian Definition is bound up with the first; the consubstantiality of Christ with man is rooted in his consubstantiality with the Father. In this way he makes it clear how much was at stake for the ancient church in the Christological controversies of the fourth and fifth centuries.

[18] *Ibid.*, 8, 15.

[19] *Ibid.*, 8, 13. Compare Lord Bacon's confession of faith: "The Three Heavenly Unities exceed all natural unities; that is, the unity of the Three Persons in the Godhead; the unity of God and man in Christ; and the unity of Christ and the Church – the Holy Ghost being the worker of both these latter unities; for by the Holy Ghost was Christ incarnate. and quickened in flesh; and by the Holy Ghost was man regenerated and quickened in the spirit." (*Works*, III, p. 123.) Here the operative factor has become spirit, and nature is left behind.

4.

Cyril of Alexandria is the last of the Greek fathers who will be cited as a witness to this doctrine. The significance of his contribution lies less in anything original he added to the development of the idea than in the fact that he was chiefly responsible for the form in which it ultimately found expression in the definition of the orthodox faith concerning the person of Christ. In numerous passages in his writings Cyril reiterates the conception, which was evidently a commonplace by his time, that the Logos, by becoming incarnate in a human body, thereby established a relation with the whole human race. This was for him the special significance of the second clause of John 1:14, "The Word became flesh and *dwelt among us*"—the Greek reads literally, "dwelt *in* us," and Cyril understood it in this sense: The Word took the flesh of an individual human being, but by that same act he came to dwell in all, in order to embrace all in the scope of his saving work: "The Word dwells in all, in the one temple which he took on our account and from us, so that having all in himself, he might reconcile all in one body to the Father" (On John 1:9).[20] Cyril expresses this universal aspect of the incarnation in a variety of ways. Sometimes he says simply, "We were all in Christ" (On John 1:9); [21] sometimes he says that the incarnate Logos "contained in himself the whole of human nature" (On John 5:2); [22] in one place he says that "the whole nature was 'enmanned' in Christ in virtue of his being man" (On John 5:2),[23] and in another that "the common person of humanity returns to life in him" (On John 1:14),[24] as if Christ by the incarnation became the subject of human nature as a whole. It is an interesting question whether this was the thought in Cyril's mind when he took the term in which the Council of Nicaea had defined the relation of the divine Christ to the Father and used it to define the relation of the human Christ to men. Usually, in speaking of the relation of Christ's manhood to ours, he expresses it in terms of likeness, e.g., "He became like us,

[20] *PG*, 73, 164.
[21] *PG*, 73, 164.
[22] *PG*, 73, 753.
[23] *PG*, 73, 753.
[24] *PG*, 73, 161.

that is, a man" (On John 12:1);[25] "He possessed likeness with us, in respect of his being man like us";[26] but in one place (at least) he uses the historic *homo-ousios.* "He became consubstantial with us, i.e., man."[27] At all events, this phrase appeared in the Formulatory of Reunion, which Cyril subscribed in 432, and thereafter it received the seal of orthodoxy in the definition of Chalcedon. There Christ is described as "consubstantial with the Father in respect to the Godhead and the same consubstantial with us in respect to the manhood."

Did the council intend the latter clause to mean anything more than what is said in the clause immediately following, "in all respects like us"? For Cyril apparently the terms were interchangeable. And, indeed, it is difficult to see how *homo-ousios* in respect to the manhood can bear the same connotation as *homo-ousios* in respect to the Godhead, at least as it was understood by Athanasius; for the *homo-ousia* of the Son with the Father meant something much more than likeness; it meant that the Son "is of the very being of the Father – so that the Father himself *is* not, does not exist, is not conceived of as having being, apart from the Son";[28] but it could hardly be said that human beings have no being apart from Christ as man. The use of *homo-ousios* in respect to the manhood may be ascribed either to Cyril's carelessness in terminology or to a weakening of the distinction between *homo-ousia* and *homoi-ousia,* which was so important in the fourth century. It is misleading in so far as it suggests that the relation of Christ as divine to the Father is identical with his relation as man to men; for there cannot be more than analogy between them. The unity of mankind in Christ (however it be conceived) cannot be the same as the unity of God.[29]

[25] *PG,* 74, 700.
[26] *Against Nestorius,* 3, 3 (*PG,* 76, 140).
[27] *Ibid.* (*PG,* 76, 141).
[28] J. F. Bethune-Baker, *Introduction to Early History of Christian Doctrine,* p. 169n. Methuen, 1951.
[29] C. C. Richardson says of the Cappadocians: "The nature of the Godhead more nearly corresponds in their thought to Aristotle's idea of

Nevertheless, Cyril's use of the term attests the strength of the motive that lay behind it.

This feature of the patristic Christology (and soteriology) has been the subject of considerable controversy in modern times. It has been vigorously attacked by some who have argued that it reduces the Christian salvation to a semimagical level and it involves philosophical notions that are unacceptable and largely unintelligible to the modern mind. On the other hand, it has been defended by some who have argued that although few or none today would be prepared to stand by the precise formulas used by the fathers, the fathers who used them were attempting to express something that is indigenous to the faith.

It will be worth our while to examine some of the charges, brought by the critics, more specifically. Three of them may be distinguished.

1. The first charge, and the one most frequently brought, is that salvation is conceived as a physical process rather than as a moral and spiritual transaction. The Greek fathers have a predilection for describing salvation as deification, and when they spell this out in terms of deliverance from corruptibility and mortality – and the acquisition of the qualities of incorruptibility and immortality – the thought appears to be that of a chemical transmutation of the substance of human nature.[30] The charge is expressed succinctly by one modern critic as follows: "There in the Greek church the Christian religion had become a deification-mystery. A permeation of our nature with the imperishable life of the divine nature was for it the heart of fellowship with God; the fact that it is our nature to be responsible persons before God and God's nature to be the Word that meets us personally in the conscience –

---

a particular, concrete existence (*prote ousia*), not to the *deutera ousia* which members of a species have in common. The *ousia* in the Godhead is *identical* in each Person: the common humanity in men is only *generic.*" *Christology of the Later Fathers* (LCC, III, p. 243).

[30] Cf. Harnack, *DG,* II[4], pp. 44 ff. Mohr, Tübingen, 1909.

that was not recognized at the decisive point." [31]

Two things may be said in defense of the fathers on this score. The first has been already mentioned: though the language of the fathers has a strongly physical ring in our ears, physical for them was not the antithesis of spiritual; rather it comprehends it within itself. The fact that they not infrequently supplement the physical with spiritual and ethical categories indicates that when they use physical terms only, they do not intend them in an exclusive (modern) sense.[32] They use physical terms in reference to the whole nature (*physis*) of man and not merely to one segment of it. This leads us to the second consideration, which is more important: If some today are astonished at a conception of salvation that has (to say the least) physical ingredients, the fathers of the ancient church would have been more astonished at one that has no such ingredients (using the word now in its restricted modern sense). For man is a physical being (in part); and a salvation that was purely moral or spiritual would be less than a full salvation. The first great struggle that the ancient church had to face was with people who sought to dissociate the whole realm of the physical from the Christian salvation; and the truly remarkable thing is that, although it stood on the soil of a culture that favored that division, the church strenuously maintained the salvation of the physical. When one church father at a later date proposed to solve the Christological problem by the ingenious theory that the divine Logos had retained the place of the human mind in the incarnate Christ, it was immediately objected that unless Christ had assumed a real human mind the salvation he wrought could not avail for the mind of man. By the same principle, and conversely, the ancient church held firmly to the position that when the incarnation was understood as the assumption of a real human body

[31] Emanual Hirsch, *Jesus Christus der Herr*, pp. 47 f. Göttingen, Vandenhoeck & Ruprecht, 1926.

[32] Cf. Athanasius, *On the Incarnation*, c. 11 (LCC, III, p. 65).

by the eternal Son, the Christian salvation must mean the salvation *of* the body, not *from* the body. It is, of course, another question whether the fathers were right in their interpretation of the physical aspect of salvation in terms of incorruptibility and immortality – assuming we could be sure we know what they meant by them – but surely we must grant that in using those terms they were endeavoring to express an inalienable aspect of the Christian salvation, and if we dislike the terms they used, we must find others to put in their place.

2. The second objection that has been raised against the patristic conception is that it tends to make the salvation of men automatic or mechanical. As Harnack puts it: "If the whole of humanity has been deified in the humanity assumed by Christ, then, from a purely logical viewpoint, it seems superfluous that anything special has to happen to the individual." [33] The salvation of the individual is accomplished over his head, or under his feet, and he is presented with it as a *fait accompli.* Though some of the fathers come near to putting it this way, yet no one ever taught a salvation that was purely automatic. One way or another, the salvation accomplished by Christ has to be appropriated by the individual. At the lowest, it has to be made known to him, and although this is sometimes spoken of as if it were equivalent to the conveyance of a factual report,[34] it was usually thought of as involving moral and spiritual factors as well.[35] Admittedly, however, the fathers have less to say about these than about the mediation of sal-

[33] *DG*, II⁴, p. 168.

[34] E.g., Hilary, *Tract. in Ps.* 143, c. 18: "By the glory of the resurrection he made his salvation known to the peoples, while they know that in him the flesh of their nature has been transformed into the substance of eternal salvation."

[35] E.g., Athanasius, *op. cit.*, c. 57, p. 110: "But for the searching of the Scriptures and true knowledge of them an honorable life is needed, and a pure soul, and that virtue which is according to Christ; so that the intellect, guiding its path by it, may be able to attain what it desires, and to comprehend it, in so far as it is accessible to human nature to learn concerning the Word of God."

vation to the individual through the sacraments; and it is in this context that they have been charged with entertaining mechanical conceptions. The sacramental doctrine of a careful theologian like Gregory of Nyssa makes it clear that for him at least the underlying concern was to establish a correspondence between the nature of salvation and the means of its communication. Something that resembles or imitates the work of Christ, the Captain of our salvation, had to be devised so that we might enjoy the benefit of it.[36] And since salvation was physical, its mediation involves physical means: " Owing to man's twofold nature, composed as it is of soul and body, those who come to salvation must be united with the Author of their life by means of both. In consequence, the soul, which has union with him by faith derives from this the means of salvation; for being united with life implies having a share in it. But it is in a different way that the body comes into intimate union with its Savior." [37] This way is the way of Baptism and the Eucharist. In Baptism the death and resurrection of Christ are " imitated," and the individual who receives it undergoes a process of rebirth. In the Eucharist, the elements that become the body of Christ by consecration are assimilated by our body (according to the Aristotelian theory of nutrition) so that it comes to share in the immortal property of his body.[38] But Gregory does not teach that the sacraments produce their effect *ex opere operato;* at least, he is explicit that without repentance and amendment of life Baptism is of no avail, and presumably the same holds good of the Eucharist: " Yet it appears to me that the instruction we have so far given is insufficient in what it teaches. We have, I think, to consider what follows Baptism. It is a point which many of those who approach its grace neglect, deluding themselves and being born in appearance only and not in reality. For the change our life undergoes through rebirth would not be a change were we to

[36] Gregory of Nyssa, *op. cit.,* c. 35 (LCC, III, p. 315).
[37] *Op. cit.,* c. 37 (LCC, III, p. 318).
[38] *Op. cit.,* c. 37 (LCC, III, pp. 318 ff.).

continue in our present state. I do not, indeed, see how a man who continues the same can be reckoned to have become different, when there is no noticeable alteration in him. For it is patent to everyone that we receive the saving birth for the purpose of renewing and changing our nature. Yet baptism produces no essential change in human nature."[39]

Gregory is not concerned to inquire how the operation of the sacraments is related to repentance and ethics; he is content to abide by the position, which appears to have been self-evident in the early period, that salvation, having been wrought for the whole nature of man, both body and soul, must be conveyed to him, and appropriated by him in the mediums both of the bodily and the spiritual.

3. The third criticism that has been brought against the patristic doctrine relates to the philosophical implicates of the conception of the humanity of Christ. This humanity, as we have seen, was conceived not merely as individual, but as generic or universal; its assumption by the eternal Son at the incarnation was understood to mean, not merely that he became a man, like other men, but that in some sense he became *man;* he entered into some kind of ontological relation with humanity as a whole. It is now generally held that this doctrine rests upon a tenet of the Platonic philosophy that has been generally rejected by modern thought, viz., that the ideas of things have a real existence that is prior to, and even superior to, the existence of the things themselves. Most of the fathers, at least in the early period, appear to have been "realists" in the sense given to the term when the great debate on the status of universals developed in the Middle Ages. They habitually speak of humanity or human nature, as if it were as real as – or even more real than – the human nature of individual men.[40]

[39] *Op. cit.*, c. 40 (LCC, III, p. 323).

[40] It should be noted, however, that the fathers made use of this piece of Platonism in order to express a doctrine that was radically opposed to that of Platonism. Platonism set up a profound antithesis between the world of ideas and the world of phenomena and held the latter

This conception is essential to the patristic doctrine of the incarnation. The humanity assumed by Christ at the incarnation is universal humanity, and universal humanity is the medium in which his work was done. None of the early fathers explicitly addresses himself to the question, in what sense universal humanity is real, nor does any undertake to explain how it is related to the humanities of individual men. The relation is certainly not that of the whole to the parts; for then any modification of humanity as a whole would be identical with the modification of humanity in all its component parts. If one's hair is dyed red, every individual hair is dyed red.[41] But none of the fathers really believed in salvation by logical necessity, however close some of them may have come to putting it like that. There was always a further step required for the salvation of individuals. This is the point at which the parallelism between Christ and Adam, which was so important in this context, tends to break down; for there could be no question of an *inclusion* of mankind in Christ such as could be conceived, in a literal sense, in Adam. The relation of mankind to Christ was no less real than the relation of mankind to Adam; but its realization in individual men involved a second and distinct step.

This duality is expressed by the fathers in various ways. It appears in its broadest and most general form in the classical statement of Irenaeus: "He became what we are in order that

---

to be deficient in reality in comparison with the former. The fathers taught that the two worlds had come together on the stage of history in the person of Christ who had embodied universal manhood in himself as an individual man. The only true Platonist among them was Apollinarius, who taught that the manhood assumed by the Logos was the eternal idea of manhood present in the mind of God; but the church rejected this doctrine and insisted that the manhood was taken "from the lump of our manhood," as Gregory of Nyssa put it.

41 For this reason Moberly's use of the term "inclusive" to describe the conception of Christ's relation to humanity in the thought of Athanasius is unfortunate (*Atonement and Personality*, p. 357); and his use of the term in his own reconstruction is misleading (p. 86).

he might make us what he is,"[42] i.e., Christ's becoming what we are is instrumental to our being made what he is, it does not coincide with it; the conception is that of a "double metathesis," as it has been called.[43] It is like that mutual indwelling of which Christ spoke in the allegory of the vine: two elements or two movements are involved, and neither excludes the other (John 15:4 ff.). The first the fathers identify with the incarnation and they speak of it usually as we have seen in terms of a relation between Christ and our nature or flesh, by which they understand that which is universal or common to mankind.[44] It is a physical or ontological relation, and, as such, it is a relation with all men *potentially*.[45] In order to become a relation with all men actually, it has to be reproduced, so to speak, in a different mode; the fathers describe this in terms of imitation, grace, participation, spirit;[46] and by these terms they evidently intend something like what we should describe as a moral and personal relation. Unless we stand in such a relation to Christ, the ontological relation established by the incarnation does not benefit us, but the ontological relation and the essential or physical conformity, which it signifies, forms the foundation or precondition of the personal relation.[47]

Since this duality is a constant feature in the thought of the fathers, however varied their individual expressions of it may be, it seems reasonable to suggest that they were striving to

[42] *Against Heresies,* 5, Pref.

[43] Cf. J. K. Mozley, *The Doctrine of the Atonement,* p. 105. Charles Scribner's Sons, 1916.

[44] Cyril of Alexandria speaks of "the common person of mankind" being raised to new life in Christ (On John 1:14, *PG,* 73, 161).

[45] Gregory of Nyssa uses this term, *op. cit.,* c. 16, p. 294.

[46] Cyril describes the purpose of the incarnation as ". . . that we might be in him and through him Sons of God, both by nature and by grace — by nature, as being in him alone, by participation and grace as being through him in the Spirit" (*PG,* 76, 1177).

[47] Cf. what Cyril says on John 1:14: "So the servile is truly liberated in Christ by ascending into mystical unity with him who bore the form of a servant, and in us by imitating him who is the one by fleshly affinity" (*PG,* 73, 161).

express what we are now accustomed to call the objective and subjective sides of the Christian salvation. The historic theories of the work of Christ, which have been propounded, have sometimes been classified under the two headings, objective and subjective; and while probably no theory is objective or subjective in an exclusive sense, they do all lean more or less to one side or the other. Viewed in this light, the patristic approach is commonly regarded as pronouncedly objective – and rightly so. Yet, as we have seen, the fathers were by no means blind to the subjective side of the matters, though they have relatively less to say about this. Their chief concern was to insist that the saving work of Christ has an objective reality prior to its subjective appropriation by us. But the most significant feature of their thought is the closeness of the relation they were able to establish between the objective and the subjective by their use of the conception of universal humanity. By their interpretation of the incarnation as the assumption of an ontological relation with mankind, the fathers were able to take the position that the work of Christ *for* man was done *in* man prior to its appropriation *by* man and thus to establish an objective ground for the work of Christ *in its vicarious character.*

CHAPTER

IV

The Humanity of Christ in Western Theology

THE KEY to the success of patristic theology in combining soteriology with Christology and, more particularly, in combining the objective and subjective sides of the work of Christ lay in the doctrine of the consubstantiality of Christ with mankind, as it is formulated in the Chalcedonian Definition. But this key is effective only so long as the philosophical concept, of which it is forged, commands assent. This was rarely the case in the West, where unqualified "realism," as it came to be called, enjoyed only a brief summer in early Scholasticism. The consequence is that although the dogmatic formulations of the ancient church have been piously preserved in the West, one vital element of their significance has been lost. The doctrine of the humanity of Christ has been understood in a different sense from that of the Definition of Chalcedon; and the proof of this is to be seen in the persistent efforts of Western theology to seek other solutions to the problem that the ancient formulation was intended to meet. This can be illustrated in three representative figures of Western theology: Anselm, Aquinas, and Calvin; all profess their acceptance of orthodox Christology, Calvin, indeed, with considerable warmth; yet in none of them does the element we have especially in view appear in its original significance and function.

Anselm's *Cur Deus Homo* is usually regarded as the first

major attempt at a theory of the atonement, and such it is; but the question propounded in its title relates to the incarnation. This was evidently the basic thing in the mind of the author. He asks, Why the God-man? not, Why did the God-man die? Now the manhood of Christ forms an essential element in the argument. It is man who has done injury to the divine honor, and therefore it is man who must make reparation. But allowing that Christ became man, the question remains how, as man, he is qualified to make reparation for the sins of all men. The answer is best given in Anselm's own words: [1]

"As it is right that man should make satisfaction for man's sin, so it is necessary that he who makes satisfaction should be the same person as the sinner, or of the same race (genus). Otherwise, neither Adam nor his race would make satisfaction for themselves. Therefore, as it was from Adam and Eve that sin spread to all men, so none but they themselves, or one born of them, ought to make satisfaction for the sin of men. And since they are unable to do it, it is necessary that it should be one born of them who does it."

Satisfaction is, strictly speaking, a personal or individual responsibility, i.e., the obligation to render it rests upon the person who committed the offense. The only concession he allows is that where the original offender is no longer in a position to render satisfaction, the responsibility may be assumed by a member of his family or race (genus), i.e., by one of his descendants. The solidarity of mankind is no longer grounded in the participation of all men in the universal of human nature, and Christ is no longer thought of as establishing an ontological relation to mankind by his assumption of an impersonal or universal human nature. The solidarity of mankind is now grounded in derivation from a single parentage, and Christ entered into it by becoming a descendant of Adam. When Anselm speaks of Christ's assumption of human

[1] Anselm, *Cur Deus Homo*, II, 8.

nature, he means, not what the Eastern church meant, but generic identity, as he makes clear when he denies the possibility of salvation for the devil and the fallen angels on the ground that, although they have a common nature, as he allows, they do not belong to a common race, in the sense that they are not derived from a single parentage.[2] The consequence of this shift, however, is that the relation of Christ to mankind is no different from that of other members of the race; there is no objective, ontological ground for the vicariousness of his saving work. This becomes clear when Anselm touches briefly on the problem of vicariousness at the end of the book: [3] it is only by a special act of grace on the part of the God-man, and almost as the solution of a dilemma, that the satisfaction receives a vicarious application. Despite the fact that God became man for the express purpose of acting in behalf of the human race, at the decisive point the God-man acts for himself alone, and the benefit of his action accrues to other men only as he of his own free will chooses to impart it to them. By interpreting the *homo-ousia*, or consubstantiality, of the incarnate Lord with our manhood as consanguinity or community of descent, Anselm left himself without an objective ground for the vicarious character of salvation which it was the intention of the ancient doctrine to supply.

The transition from East to West is marked with special clarity in Thomas Aquinas, because he shows a much deeper awareness of the problem than Anselm or any of his predecessors, and discusses it with his customary thoroughness. Aquinas deliberately rejects the patristic doctrine of the universality of the humanity of Christ on philosophical grounds. He explores the question of Christ's assumption of human nature from every angle.[4] Is it permissible to say that the divine person assumed "man" (*homo*)? [5] Yes, perhaps in popular speech where man is used loosely as synonymous with human nature;

[2] *Op. cit.*, II, 21.
[3] *Op. cit.*, II, 19.
[4] S. *T.*, III, Q. 4.
[5] S. *T.*, III, Q. 4, A. 3.

but strictly speaking, "man" connotes human nature complete with personality; and it smacks of Nestorianism to say that the Word assumed a human person. Can it then be said that the Son of God assumed human nature in the abstract? [6] No; for human nature, whether it be regarded as having being as a Platonic idea or as existing as an idea in the mind of God or man, lacks the sensible material element of flesh and bones that belongs to its definition.[7] Human nature only becomes real in individual concretion. The Word then assumed human nature, not in the universal but in the individual – it being always borne in mind that the human nature he assumed did not have its individual subsistence in itself but achieved it in the person of the Word.[8] In this Thomas is taking the position taken previously by the Damascene, whose authority he invokes.[9] He then asks whether the vicarious scope of the work of Christ obliges us to understand the incarnation as the assumption of human nature by the Word in all individuals. Would this not be the quickest way to achieve the purpose, and the way most consonant with love, whose property it is to dispense itself to others? Aquinas counters this with an appeal to the principle of economy; it is the mark of a wise man not to use a multitude of means when he can accomplish his purpose by one. In fact, says Aquinas, the two methods are incompatible: "The love of God toward men is manifested not only in the actual assumption of human nature but chiefly by what he suffered in human nature for other men . . . and there would be no room for this, if he had assumed human nature in all men." [10] The Greek fathers had sought to build a bridge between the work of Christ *for* us and its appropriation *by* us with the doctrine of Christ incarnate *in* us; but to Aquinas this bridge had become a dam; it seemed to him that the idea

[6] S. *T.*, III, Q. 4, A. 4.
[7] *Ibid., resp.*
[8] S. *T.*, III, Q. 2, A. 2 and 3.
[9] John of Damascus, *De Orth. Fide,* III, 11.
[10] S. *T.*, III, Q. 4, A. 5 ad 2.

of the universal or inclusive humanity of Christ would destroy the vicarious character of his work, which is intentional rather than natural: "The Son of God became incarnate as the common Savior of all men, not by community of genus or species, such as belongs to a nature distinct from individuals, but by community of cause, inasmuch as the Son of God became incarnate for the sake of universal human salvation." [11]

But how can the vicarious intention acquire universal scope? Aquinas finds the answer in the doctrine of the grace given to Christ as head of the church. There are in Christ three distinct graces: there is the grace given to him as an individual (*gratia habitualis*); there is the grace of the hypostatic union (*gratia unionis*); and to crown all, there is the superabundant fullness of grace given to him as head of the church (*gratia fontalis*): "For the soul of Christ received grace in such wise that it should be poured from it to other men . . . grace was bestowed on him as the universal principle in the class of those who have grace." [12] The question is whether Christ is head of the church as man. Aquinas examines the metaphor of the body and defines the qualifications of headship as order (or superiority), perfection, and power (i.e., the power to regulate and influence the rest of the body); he concludes that these properties pertain to Christ – but spiritually. It is in fact the grace of headship that constitutes Christ the head of the church, and thus it is grounded in his divinity rather than in his humanity; for "to give grace or the Holy Spirit pertains to Christ as God fundamentally (or originally, *auctoritative*); it pertains to him as man instrumentally, inasmuch as his humanity is the instrument of his divinity." [13] Even the instrumental role that he here concedes to the humanity is hard to find. It does not mean that his humanity constitutes the medium through which

[11] *Ibid.,* ad 1. Thomas is not quite consistent, however, when he argues later that the sufferings of Christ were universal in *genus* (though not in *species*). S. *T.*, III, Q. 46, A. 5.

[12] S. *T.*, III, Q. 8, A. 1 ad 1.

[13] S. *T.*, III, Q. 8, A. 1 ad 1.

the benefits of his saving work are transmitted to us. "The Passion of Christ, although corporal, has spiritual power from the divinity that is united with it: and so it imparts its efficacy by spiritual contact, i.e., by faith and the sacrament of faith." [14] In effect, it may be said, Aquinas transposes the whole question from the key of nature to that of grace – and here *gratia tollit naturam.* The positive role of the humanity in the Christology of Aquinas is hard to discern; it certainly plays no decisive part in constituting the basis for the vicarious efficacy of the work of Christ; for "it is by the power of the divinity that his actions were salutary for us." [15] By the same token Aquinas has transferred the question from the context of the doctrine of the incarnation to that of the doctrine of the church. He views the solidarity of Christ with us ecclesiologically rather than ontologically, and he retains this view even when the matter is presented in its universal aspect. The ecclesiological view might be thought to impose a limitation upon the solidarity of Christ with mankind and thus upon the scope of his vicarious work, but Aquinas gets round the difficulty with the argument that the grace which Christ has as head of the church is sufficiently powerful to make him the head of all men: "Unbelievers, although not of the church in fact, are nevertheless of the church potentially. This potentiality is grounded on two things: (1) the power of Christ, which is sufficient for the salvation of the entire human race, and (2) the freedom of the will." [16]

A similar failure to integrate Christology with soteriology can be seen in Calvin. Calvin was an ardent champion of Christological orthodoxy and evidently attached a profound significance to Christ's consubstantiality with man; it receives a marked emphasis in his treatment of the incarnation. For him, as for Anselm, Christ's assumption of human nature is an essential precondition of his mediatorial work, and its universal

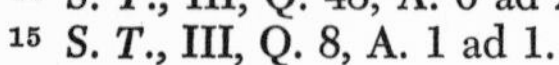

[14] S. *T.*, III, Q. 48, A. 6 ad 2.
[15] S. *T.*, III, Q. 8, A. 1 ad 1.
[16] S. *T.*, III, Q. 8, A. 3 ad 1.

aspect is repeatedly stressed. Calvin speaks of it in language that reveals a profound sympathy with ancient patristic formulations: " It was necessary that the Son of God should become Immanuel, God with us, for this reason that there might be a mutual union and coalition between his divinity and the nature of man." [17] It is by this unity of nature he was entitled to act in place of man and render to God that which was required of man: " Our Lord then came forward as true man; he put on the person of Adam and assumed his name, to act as his substitute in obediently submitting to the Father, to present our flesh as the price of satisfaction to the just judgment of God and in the same flesh to pay the penalty which we had deserved." [18] Moreover, " our common nature is the pledge of our fellowship with the Son of God." Relying on this pledge, " we are confident that we are the children of God," and that Christ's " victory and triumph are ours." [19]

In all of this Calvin appears to be laying an objective foundation for the vicariousness of the work of Christ. When we turn to the third book of the *Institutes,* however, we note with surprise that not a trace of it remains. The Christ who, we learned earlier, came and joined himself to us and took our nature and put on the person of Adam in order that he might act for us, has now got separated from us and is outside us, and so long as he remains so, " all that he suffered and achieved for the salvation of the human race is of no avail and no significance to us. To communicate to us what he has received from the Father he must become ours and dwell in us." [20] Calvin is not here referring back to the relation established by the incarnation of Christ in our nature, as a reader of his words might be justified in supposing. He is introducing an entirely

[17] *Inst.* II, 12. 1.

[18] *Inst.* II, 12. 3.

[19] *Ibid.* Calvin also speaks of a substantial community (or sharing of substance) between Christ and us. Cf. his Commentaries on Gal. 2:20; Eph. 5:29.

[20] *Inst.* III, 1. 1.

new theme, the union of Christ and believers, as head and members in his body, the church. This is a different union from that which was established between Christ and humanity by the incarnation. The incarnate union was based on Christ's possession of a common nature with us; the union of which Calvin now speaks is based on the gift of the Holy Spirit: "the Holy Spirit is the bond by which Christ efficaciously unites us to himself."[21]

As we read what Calvin has to say about the spiritual union between Christ and his church – and this is a theme on which he loves to dilate–it becomes difficult to believe that any meaning is left to the natural relation between Christ and humanity of which he spoke in the earlier context. The difficulty is intensified by two other features of Calvin's thought. The first is the doctrine of election, according to which the identity of those who are to be beneficiaries of Christ's saving work is determined, not by community of nature, but by the inscrutable divine decree. The other is his polemic against Osiander. Osiander propounded the doctrine that in justification we are not only declared righteous, but we are made substantially or essentially righteous, because the essence of Christ is infused into us or blended with ours. This would seem to be only the logical complement of Christ's assumption of our human nature by the incarnation, as Calvin himself understood it; but he pronounced Osiander's doctrine "monstrous."[22] He refused to entertain the thought that our nature was transformed in consequence of its having been worn by Christ,[23] and insisted that what Christ accomplished for us becomes ours only by imputation.[24]

[21] *Ibid.*

[22] *Inst.* III, 11. 5 ff.

[23] But he was not able to avoid it completely; in his comment on II Peter 1:4 ("partakers of the divine nature" – a passage of immense significance in Eastern theology) he writes: "Let us observe that this is the purpose of the gospel, to make us conformed to God, that is, as it were, to be deified, so to speak" (*quasi deificari, ut ita loquamur*).

[24] *Inst.* III, 11. 2.

It is evident that Calvin has in effect moved away from the classical incarnational conception of the relation of Christ to humanity, in spite of the very sympathetic attitude toward it that he showed in his treatment of the incarnation. Calvin's attempt to combine the norms of the Eastern and Western churches succeeded only in demonstrating the depth of the difference between them. The classical doctrine, which conceived the relation of Christ to humanity in terms of nature, could not meet the needs of the Protestant Reformation, which insisted on a relation at the level of personality, a relation of personal encounter and personal response. When the Reformers proceeded to elaborate their doctrine of the Christian salvation, they abandoned the metaphysical categories of the classical Christology in favor of legal categories, like imputation; because these presuppose a context of personal relations. But the criticisms to which such ideas as imputation have been exposed show that the more the gospel is interpreted in terms of persons rather than natures, the more difficult it becomes to account for its vicarious character. The vicarious character of the work of Christ has been a persistent problem in the Protestant thought.

An early attempt to find a solution to the problem within a framework of legal categories was made by the federal theology, which sought to base the vicarious nature of the work of Christ in his relation to men (or to the elect) as their federal head. The federal theologians did usually try to leave some significance to consubstantiality, but in effect it was swallowed up in confederation; for the distinctive thing about this theology is not that it employed the covenant idea, which is soundly Biblical, but that it projected the idea back into the eternal order and grounded the salvation of mankind in the covenant made between the Father and the Son before the foundation of the world. Confederation was thus made more ultimate than consubstantiality; Christ's assumption of our nature was part of his equipment for the office of Mediator, but the office itself was ascribed to him solely by divine appointment.[25]

The federal theology, a characteristic product of a legally minded age, maintained its appeal so long as the minds of men were responsive to the legal concepts and categories with which it operated. Its appeal began to decline toward the closing years of the eighteenth century. The rationalist and romantic movements of that period were evidences of a revolution in men's ways of thinking that had a profound influence in theology and that demanded restatement of the gospel in another kind of concepts and categories.

[25] Cf. Westminster Confession, Ch. VIII. In the classical doctrine the mediation of Christ is "an office which belongs to him by nature, and results from the constitution of his being." (R. S. Wilberforce, *The Doctrine of the Incarnation,* p. 172. Hooker and Co., Philadelphia, 1849.)

CHAPTER

V

The Universality of Christ in Modern Theology

WHEN we survey the latest phase of Christological thought, which extends over the last two hundred years, it becomes apparent that the notion of the consubstantiality of Christ with mankind, although it is remote from the minds of most thinkers in this period, forms the concealed or unconscious theme of much of the discussion; in other words, much of the ferment in Christology, which was set in motion by rationalist criticism in the latter part of the eighteenth century, took place in or around the vacuum resulting from the virtual disappearance of the notion from the European mind. The distinctive feature of the rationalist critique of religion was not its insistence on rationality, but the sharp distinction it drew between the rational and the historical. The objection to orthodox Christianity was not that its doctrines were contrary to reason, but that they were based on, and derived their authority from, historical events of the past. The doctrines themselves were rational enough; but their intrinsic rationality was concealed or lost when they were enclosed in a historical matrix. Rationalism undertook to demonstrate that the doctrines of religion were grounded in the principles and ideals of reason and could therefore be accepted universally by autonomous reason. The orthodox position which based the truths of faith on historical grounds was rejected principally for three reasons: (1) Historical events could not be apprehended with the same degree of certainty and conviction as rational truths. They could not bear the weight that orthodoxy laid upon them unless they were accepted on authority, and that was inconsistent with the autonomy of reason. The point was expressed by Lessing in the oft-quoted words, "Contingent truths of history can never become the proof of necessary truths of reason."[1] (2) The nascent science of historical criticism was beginning to discover the difficulty of achieving certainty about historical events, especially those belonging to the remote past. This is what Lessing had in mind when he spoke, in the context of the words just quoted, of "the ugly, broad ditch" (*der garstige breite Graben*) that separates Christ and the apostles from us, and that he found it impossible to leap over. (3) It came to be felt that if religious truth were bound up with historical truth, its relevance would be restricted to those who belonged to a particular historical tradition and its universality would be negated.

This was a point made by Kant in his *Religion Within the Limits of Mere Reason,* which may be regarded as the classical expression of the rationalist critique of religion. To Kant the validity of religion was bound up with its universal significance, and this was incompatible with its being attached to any historical event or person. Kant deals with the question of the place of Christ in Christianity in the second section of his work. He refused to allow him the place that orthodoxy ascribes to him; for to make Christ the object of faith would, in his view, restrict faith to those who were able to accept the historical records on which it is based. Kant sees a radical difference between such history-faith, as he calls it, and religious faith, which is equivalent to rational faith. Religious faith is faith in the moral ideal or the idea of mankind in its complete moral perfection, and, as such, it may be held with complete indifference to history. Belief in the existence of the historical

[1] *Beweis des Geistes und der Kraft,* Theol. Schriften, ed. by Gross, II, 2, p. 12.

Christ is not necessary to belief in the principles of Christianity. It may fulfill an instrumental function in relation to it; the figure of the historical Christ may help to represent the idea of the moral perfection of mankind, which is the real object of the purpose of God, and his example may incite us to pursue it. But to a truly rational faith the historical can be no more than the "vehicle" (a favorite term with Kant here) of the ideal. It is only by virtue of his relation to the idea, whether as symbol or example or pioneer, that Kant is able to concede the possibility of a universal significance to the person of the historical Christ. This meager concession points up the vacuum that had been left by the loss of the notion of the solidarity of Christ with mankind.

Much of the thought of the ensuing period may be read as a series of efforts to reunite the principle of Christianity with the person of Christ, which rationalism had severed, and so to recover for the person of Christ a significance as universal as the principle of the faith with which he was connected. The development took place in the main along two lines which were originated by the two great figures of the early nineteenth century, Hegel and Schleiermacher.

Hegel sought to carry forward and complete the rationalization of religion that had been begun by Kant. He differed from Kant chiefly in two respects: (1) His conception of religion was much broader and more comprehensive; whereas religion for Kant was virtually equivalent to ethics, it was for Hegel a variant form of metaphysics. (2) Hegel thought that his rationalized version brought out the real and essential meaning of Christianity. His attitude to Christianity was more positive and friendly than that of Kant; whereas the idea of religion in Kant's reductionist program is clearly deistic, Hegel found the clues to his reinterpretation in the Christian doctrines of the Trinity, the incarnation, and the atonement.

Hegel appeared to give the historical person of Christ a central place in his system. He viewed reality as the self-realization of the absolute Spirit, or God, by the dialectical process in which he goes out from himself and returns to himself. The ultimate truth, or it would be better to say the theme, of the whole is the identity of the absolute and the finite spirit (or of God and man) – an identity that does not exclude distinction but that is realized by the dialectical process of the reconciliation of contraries. This was to him the true meaning of the Christian doctrines of the God-man and the atonement; but while orthodox Christianity expresses it in imaginative form, its truth can be seen only if it is restated in metaphysical form. The historical fact of Christ has then a symbolic significance; its meaning is found, not in itself, but in the larger idea to which it points.

Hegel purported to be "explaining" Christianity – and his explanation was received with considerable satisfaction in some quarters – but the question is whether he has not explained it away. The crucial question concerns the place of the historical Christ in the system: does he fill an essential and indispensable role, or is he ultimately expendable? On this question the followers of Hegel split into two camps. The left-wing Hegelians, as they were called, inclined to the view that in exposing the true idea of God-manhood Hegel had undermined the orthodox faith concerning the person of the God-man. These were probably the true interpreters of the mind of the master; for though Hegel himself had been willing to concede to the historical Christ the distinction of having been the first to perceive the great truth of the unity of God and man, the truth stands independently of him: there is no essential connection between the universal idea and the particular person, and, indeed, they were felt to be incompatible. Left-wing Hegelianism was brought to its logical conclusion by David Friedrich Strauss who completely severed the idea from the history. Strauss reduced the gospel history to the status of myth, not by literal and historical criticism, but simply because of his antecedent conviction that a universal idea, by its very nature, cannot be anchored to a single, historical person. If the idea is to be deployed in history, it requires the whole canvas, the totality of individuals; it is too great to be contained in one. "It is not at all the manner of the idea to realize itself by pouring all its fullness into one specimen and keeping it from all others; it loves rather to spread out its riches in a multiplicity of specimens which complement one another." [2] Orthodox Christianity confronted Strauss with what has been called "the scandal of particularity" in an insuperable way. He saw a radical incompatibility between the idea of the God-manhood and the unique claims that were made for the historical Christ, and he felt, paradoxically, that the truth of the Christological dogma could be conserved only if it were dissociated from the person of Christ; for the historical, individual Christ could not bear the universal significance which the dogma assigned to him: "No individual at all, and, in particular, no historical starting point can be at the same time archetypal (*urbildlich*)." [3]

The right-wing Hegelians were a group of theologians who had been profoundly stimulated by the Hegelian philosophy and who strove to establish an essential connection between the truth of the idea and the person of the historical Christ. They held to the Hegelian position regarding the universal scope of the idea of God-manhood, but they sought to deduce from the principles of the system itself the necessity of an individual God-man. Some extended the dialectic and argued that the universal idea must first manifest itself in an individual; others tried to make the system less inhospitable to the concept of personality by arguing that personality is a unity of both universal and particular elements and that the general notion of mankind could only receive personification in a single, complete personality; others again argued that the idea of God-manhood, as the result of the dialectical movement of reconciliation, must first be realized in an individual God-man,

[2] Strauss, *Leben Jesu,* II, pp. 734 f.

[3] *Op. cit.,* p. 717.

from whom, as its bearer, its universal realization is mediated.[4] In their various ways all were seeking a philosophical equivalent for the traditional, theological doctrine of Christ as the second Adam or the head and representative of mankind. And although it is doubtful whether such an equivalent can be found in terms of authentic Hegelianism, Hegelianism must be given the credit for having raised the question in such a way as to compel theologians, and not only those of Hegelian sympathies, to consider it anew. The problem of the universal significance of Christ recurs repeatedly in the thought of the ensuing period.

~

The differences between Hegel and Schleiermacher are not so great as the similarity of their basic conceptions. Both of them begin with a notion of the essence of religion, which is conceived in general terms, and then find themselves confronted with the problem of relating the general idea to the particular person of Christ. The differences between them, which lie within this common area of agreement, are principally two: (1) Whereas Hegel was interested only in the rational articulation of the idea of religion, Schleiermacher was concerned with the conscious experience of it; and so (2), whereas Hegel proceeded deductively from the idea to the phenomena of religion, Schleiermacher employed the inductive method; he made the human experience of religion his starting point and sought from that to reach its ideal essence.

The Christian-religious experience, according to Schleiermacher, is a unique enhancement of our consciousness of God. This experience occurs within the context of the Christian community, but cannot be derived from forces immanent in the community. Its source is Christ. The question is how an

[4] A full account of the thought of some of the leading figures (which is often highly complex and abstruse) is given by Dorner in his *History of the Doctrine of the Person of Christ,* Division II, Vol. 3, pp. 121–173. The above summary is based on that of Luthardt in his *Kompendium der Dogmatik* (11th edit.), p. 233, Dörffling and Franke, Leipzig, 1914.

experience of this kind can be derived from a particular historical person and Schleiermacher's answer is that the experience was present in Christ in such a unique degree that it communicates itself from him to others. The consciousness of God and (its negative counterpart) the absence of sin in him were of such a perfection and potency as to constitute "a veritable being of God in him."[5] And on this account he is more than a pattern or example (*Vorbild*) for us, he is the archetype (*Urbild*), i.e., the type or pattern that has the power of reproducing itself in others. It is by this concept, which plays a decisive role in his Christology, that Schleiermacher attempts to unite the universal principle with the historical person.

There are attractive features in this approach, which Schleiermacher might have developed to better advantage. When he treats of the communication of the blessedness of Christ to the Christian community, it becomes doubtful if he is thinking of anything more than the extension of a historical influence, as if Christ merely delivered the initial impulse to a movement that continues by the momentum derived from it. It is not the living Christ, but rather the image or picture (*Bild*) of Christ that lives on in the church; and we are left in some doubt whether the significance of Christ for the church is fundamentally different from that of, say, George Washington for the American people.

Nevertheless, Schleiermacher deserves credit for having focussed attention upon the person of Christ at a time when it was in danger of being lost in a fog of abstract ideas, and for having sought the clue to his universal significance in the historical experience of his life.

~

The discussion of the problem of the universal significance of Christ was continued in the theology of the English-speak-

[5] Schleiermacher, *The Christian Faith,* § 94 (ET, p. 385). T. & T. Clark, 1928.

ing world mainly in the direction pointed by Schleiermacher. Schleiermacher had rejected the view that the solution was to be found in the ontological constitution of his person apart from consideration of his work, as the traditional separation of the two doctrines seemed to imply. He insisted that we cannot determine what Christ *is* except in the light of what he *does:* "The peculiar activity and the exclusive dignity of the Redeemer imply each other, and are inseparably one in the self-consciousness of believers." [6] This empirical approach was congenial to the temper of the English-speaking world, and it was widely followed in the nineteenth century — not indeed in conscious dependence on Schleiermacher; it must be viewed rather as a spontaneous development. It took the form of a remarkable series of fresh studies of the atonement.

The occasion for the reopening of this question was the breakdown of the penal-substitutionary theory, which had been accepted for centuries. The juridical categories, in which the theory is cast, lost that power of conviction over the minds of men which they appear to have enjoyed in the seventeenth century. The nineteenth century was marked by a decided turning away from legal to ethical categories, and this ethical sensitivity, which may be traced to Kant, had a profound influence in theology. The theology of the period in England and America is characterized by the determination to translate the gospel into ethical concepts and categories, and it was inevitable that the effort should be concentrated on the central doctrine of the atoning work of Christ. But perhaps the most significant feature of this phase of theology was that although the ethical approach brought some immediate advantages, it tended to throw into relief the problem of the universal scope of the atonement, and some of its ablest representatives found themselves driven back to the incarnational theology of the ancient church.

This may be illustrated by two famous books which represent in classical form the moralizing program of nineteenth

[6] *Op. cit.,* § 92.

century theology. The first is McLeod Campbell's book *The Nature of the Atonement,* which appeared in 1856. There are several sides to the argument that is developed in this profound and difficult book, but the core of it lies in Campbell's conception of the content of the atoning sacrifice that Christ offered to the Father for the sins of men. His objection to the accepted theory, which saw the content of the atoning sacrifice in the sufferings of Christ, was that it failed to show any reason why suffering as such should have atoning virtue. The atoning virtue, he contended, must be sought, not in the sufferings as such, but in the mind and attitude that lay behind them; and this led him to his distinctive conception that the sufferings of Christ are the expression of the mind of God upon the sins of men on the one hand, and the human response of a perfect confession of sin and a perfect repentance for sin on the other. It was not enough, he argued, that the penal consequences of sin should be borne in the name of humanity; for this did not go to the heart of the matter. It was necessary that the divine judgment on human sin should be endorsed in the name of humanity; there had to be " a perfect confession of our sins . . . a perfect Amen in humanity to the judgment of God on the sin of man. Such an Amen was due in the truth of things."[7]

This novel conception was received with some bewilderment. " The theory," wrote A. B. Bruce, in 1874, " has been treated by critics of all schools as the eccentricity of a devout author, who, dissatisfied with the traditional theory, has substituted in its place another, involving not only greater difficulty, but even something very like absurdity. The idea of a confession made by a perfectly holy being, involving *all* the elements of a perfect repentance, *except* the personal consciousness of sin, is certainly absurd enough."[8] Critics have continued to

[7] Campbell, *The Nature of the Atonement* (1st edit.), p. 134; (5th edit., p. 117). The Macmillan Company, 1856.

[8] Bruce, *The Humiliation of Christ* (5th edit.), p. 318. T. & T. Clark, 1914.

stumble at that stumbling stone. The author of a recent survey of modern theories of the atonement fixes on it as "probably the most difficult as well as the weakest point" in theories of this type: "We are impelled to raise the question whether it is psychologically and spiritually possible for one man to be penitent instead of, or on behalf of, another, and in such a way as to make his penitence efficacious to new life and to a reconciliation with God. Penitence must be each man's own in the sense in which every action of his is his own."[9] The difficulty of conceiving a vicarious repentance psychologically, to which this writer refers, is an index of the fact that the more the work of Christ is interpreted in ethical terms, the more difficult it becomes to account for its vicarious character. If the principle of personal or individual responsibility is absolutized, as it tends to be in post-Kantian ethics, vicarious action is not only impossible, but the very idea of it is unethical. It is this difficulty which prompted some to seek a solution in the categories of the traditional Christology; it is significant that various attempts have been made in the last hundred years to rehabilitate the classical doctrine of the incarnation.

The issue was raised by one of the original reviewers of Campbell's book, who pointed out that the doctrine of mediation was incompatible with modern individualism and presupposed a "realistic" conception of the universal manhood of Christ.[10] Campbell replied that he had no conception of such a realism and gave it as his opinion that he had unconsciously, but safely, steered a middle course between individualism and realism, which he likened to Scylla and Charybdis.[11] It is noteworthy, however, that his own mind was led to a profounder realization of the connection between the atonement and the incarnation. In the introduction to the second edition he de-

[9] T. Hywel Hughes, *The Atonement,* p. 135. Allen and Unwin, 1949.
[10] See the note appended to the second edition of *The Nature of the Atonement.*
[11] *Op. cit.* (5th edit.), p. 346.

clared that the incarnation is "the primary and highest fact in the history of God's relation to man," and that the atonement can only be understood in the light of it. He gave this account of his own approach: "Assuming the incarnation, I have sought to realize the divine mind in Christ as perfect Sonship toward God and perfect Brotherhood toward men, and, doing so, the incarnation has appeared developing itself naturally and necessarily as the atonement."[12]

McLeod Campbell left the matter with this brief allusion and did not go on to demonstrate how the atonement, as he understood it, was bound up with the incarnation. A more systematic attempt to do so was made by R. C. Moberly in his book *Atonement and Personality,* which was published in 1901. Moberly took much the same view as Campbell of the content of Christ's atoning work, but he sought to establish it on a firmer foundation by relating it more definitely to the doctrine of the incarnation. The possibility of vicarious penitence, he argued, depends, not on its psychological plausibility — although he pleaded that human experience showed it was not so implausible as it has sometimes been represented — but on the catholic Christology with its affirmation of the full and perfect divinity and humanity of Christ. When we affirm the divinity of Christ, he pointed out, we mean that Christ is God identically, not generically, and he contended that the humanity of Christ must be understood in an analogous way: "If he might have been, yet he certainly was not, a man only, amongst men. His relation to the human race is not that he was another specimen, differing, by being another, from everyone except himself. His relation to the race was not a differentiating but a consummating relation. He was not generically, but inclusively man."[13] Moberly was concerned to establish the vicarious power of Christ's atoning work on an objective

[12] *Op. cit.,* p. xvii. It is not clear that Campbell fully appreciated the point of the criticism.

[13] R. C. Moberly, *Atonement and Personality,* p. 86. John Murray, London, 1901.

ground, prior to its "translation into the subjective"[14] (i.e., the faith and experience of believers), and such a ground, he thought, was given in the classical view of the relation of the incarnate Lord to humanity, a relation that made it possible to say that his "atoning acts were not so much acts done by him instead of us, as acts, which, in his doing them, we all did."[15]

The revival of interest in the classical Christology was not confined to Moberly. Others were led in the same direction, especially within the Anglican communion – and this is natural, since Anglicans have always cherished a greater venera-

[14] *Op. cit.*, p. 281.

[15] *Op. cit.*, p. 344. There is, however, a significant difference between Moberly and the ancient fathers, which emerges in his further development of the idea of the universal or "inclusive" humanity of Christ. To them it was based in Christ's consubstantiality with men; Christ became universal man by being incarnate in the substance of humanity. Moberly wished to establish it on a spiritual ground. Thus, while he declares that the relation of Adam to humanity is the only one with which that of Christ can be compared, he strongly emphasizes the difference between them: "The one is a fleshly relation, the other a spiritual. The one works automatically, materially, mechanically. The other is realized in a different sphere, and depends upon other than material conditions" (*op. cit.*, p. 89; cf. the summary by William Temple in *Foundations*, p. 253). It is, in fact, the relation that is established by the gift of the Spirit at Pentecost; Moberly saw in this what he called "the heart of the matter": "What Jesus in himself suffered, or did, on Calvary, you may perhaps explain in terms of Calvary. . . . But the relation of what he did to us, its working, its reality for us and in us, you can only explain at all in terms of Pentecost" (*op. cit.*, p. 151). Although it may be readily granted that there is value in Moberly's treatment of the gift and work of the Spirit as the real consummation of the atonement, it should be noted that in basing the relation of Christ to humanity on this ground he has departed from the position of the ancient church in precisely the same way as Calvin. Where he says, "Calvary without Pentecost would not be an atonement to us" (*op. cit.*, p. 152), they would have said, "Calvary without Bethlehem." To them the work of Christ on Calvary has atoning virtue for us because of the relation to us in which he already stands by the incarnation. But in spite of his efforts to link the atonement with the incarnation, Moberly, like Anselm, leaves Christ at the decisive point to act alone, and his act acquires vicarious effect only by a relation that is established subsequently. It is significant that Moberly's view is sometimes classified among subjective theories (cf. J. K. Mozley, *The Doctrine of the Atonement*, p. 195).

tion for the fathers of the ancient church than has been customary in Protestantism. Moberly was followed closely by William Temple and by his own son, W. H. Moberly, in their contribution to *Foundations*.[16] A parallel and apparently spontaneous development in American Anglicanism found its spokesman in W. P. Du Bose, who kept recurring to the theme in several of his books. The incarnation, he said, "was in humanity and not only in man";[17] and in support of this position he appealed to the ancient doctrines of *anhypostasia* and *enhypostasia*. *Anhypostasia* is defined by D. M. Baillie as "the ancient doctrine that Christ is not a human person, but a divine person who assumed human nature without assuming human personality";[18] it is sometimes referred to as the doctrine of the "impersonal humanity" of Christ. *Enhypostasia* is the idea put forward by Leontius of Byzantium that "the humanity of Christ, while not impersonal, can be described as not having *independent* personality, but being personal in the Logos."[19] It is obvious that these conceptions, separately or in combination, readily lend themselves to use in support of the doctrine of the universal significance of the person of Christ, although it is doubtful if this formed any part of the original intention behind their formulation. According to Dorner, it was a German theologian called Philippi who "introduced under the impersonality of the humanity of Christ the meaning that Christ is not an individual man, but that humanity in general was assumed by him."[20] But a similar conception was advanced in Scotland at an earlier date by Erskine of Linlathen, to whom, perhaps, this school of thought owes a deeper debt than is commonly acknowledged. His book on the atonement,

[16] See pp. 252 and 322 f.

[17] W. P. Du Bose, *High Priesthood and Sacrifice*, p. 217. Longmans, 1908.

[18] D. M. Baillie, *op. cit.*, p. 85.

[19] *Op. cit.*, p. 90.

[20] I. A. Dorner, *System of Christian Doctrine*, III, p. 254n2. T. & T. Clark, 1885.

The Brazen Serpent, which was published in 1831, anticipates much of the thought of McLeod Campbell and Moberly. In it he wrote: "We are all of one flesh, but we are kept separate, and walled off, from each other, by our being individual persons. The individual personality gives us that feeling of distinct responsibility which, in great measure, detaches us from the actions of others, as if we had nothing to do with them. But Jesus had no human personality. He had the human nature under the personality of the Son of God. And so his human nature was more open to the commonness of man – for the divine, whilst it separated him from sinners, in point of sin, united him to them in love. And thus the sins of other men were to Jesus what the affections and lusts of his own particular flesh are to each individual believer."[21] Moberly rejected *anhypostasia;* he insisted that Christ is a person, and a human person at that. But he favored *enhypostasia:* "The root and origin of his personality may not be human," he wrote, and, more categorically: "There was in him no impersonal humanity (which is impossible); but a human nature and character which were personal because they were now the method and condition of his own personality."[22] It appears also to have been the *enhypostasia,* rather than the *anhypostasia,* with

[21] Thomas Erskine, *The Brazen Serpent,* pp. 71 f. Waugh & Innes, 1831. Principal Tulloch, who knew him personally, wrote of Erskine: "What is most remarkable to a student nowadays in [Erskine] is the lack of historical knowledge in dealing with Christian dogma. . . . He has no consciousness of the real relation of his views to the older theology . . . or again how far he was merely reviving, or bringing forth anew, aspects of ancient doctrine. . . . A larger acquaintance with the history of theological opinion would have been able to see that a good deal of his distinctive teaching was not new in the thought of the church" (*Movements of Religious Thought in Britain During the Nineteenth Century,* pp. 143 ff. Charles Scribner's Sons, 1885). The language of the passage cited above makes it difficult to believe that Erskine was not acquainted with the ecclesiastical doctrines of *anhypostasia* and *enhypostasia* and that he was merely constructing them out of his own head.

[22] R. C. Moberly, *op. cit.,* p. 94.

which Du Bose was principally concerned, when he wrote: "The universality of our Lord's humanity is only explicable upon the fact that his personality is a divine one. It is only God in it that can make it applicable to all or the truth of all. . . . The concrete universal of humanity which may be found in Jesus Christ belongs to it not as humanity but as God in humanity. It is God in it which makes that particular humanity of our Lord, his holiness, his righteousness, his life, valid and available for all."[23] And finally Dr. H. M. Relton also argues in his monograph on the *enhypostasia* that the union of the particular person and the universal principle in Christ can be accounted for only in terms of this doctrine, although he seems to despair of making the doctrine intelligible in itself: "However incredible or logically impossible such a phenomenon may appear, the fact remains that in the Person of Jesus Christ is revealed one who was a particular man, and yet the universal man; one, moreover, whose consciousness was at once limited and unlimited, finite and circumscribed yet infinite and uncircumscribed in its range, human and yet divine, divine and yet human. If we say that it is intellectually inconceivable and historically impossible, the facts reprove us. Faith can grasp it. The Gospels record it. Is there any hypothesis which will cover it? The doctrine of the *enhypostasia* is the one that we venture to suggest. It is based on grounds that make it at least conceivable to the human mind. It does not solve the problem, because the problem is ultimately insolvable by any finite mind. It postulates a logical impossibility – the particular cannot embody its own universal. But the Person of Christ is the bankruptcy of human logic."[24] It may be felt that the difficulty of the conception is more psychological than logical; for it seems impossible to spell it out

[23] W. P. Du Bose, *The Gospel According to St. Paul*, pp. 297 ff. Longmans, 1907.

[24] H. M. Relton, *A Study in Christology*, p. 265. S. P. C. K., London, 1917.

in terms of psychology without falling into something very like Apollinarianism. If the divine "person," who assumed human nature without assuming human personality, is taken in the psychological sense as a center of consciousness or subject of experience, the doctrine becomes irreconcilable with the full humanity of Christ, since a human nature is inconceivable without a human personal subject. Personality is an essential element of humanity; and if Christ were not a human person, he would not be truly man, he would not really be "consubstantial with us as regards the manhood." However, since it was precisely for denying the presence of a human consciousness in Christ that Apollinarius was condemned, it is clear that the doctrine of the "impersonal humanity" cannot have been intended in this sense. It has often been pointed out that the term *hypostasis* in the classical Christology bears a different meaning from "person" in modern speech; E. L. Mascall, indeed, goes so far as to suggest that it was deliberately chosen in order to remove the problem from the sphere of psychology altogether. The classical Christology, he insists, was formulated in ontological terms, and it cannot be understood unless we resist the temptation to transpose it to a psychological key. His book *Christ, the Christian and the Church,* which has for its subtitle "A Study of the Incarnation and Its Consequences," is an attempt to restate, or reinterpret, the doctrine of the incarnation with strict regard to the ontological character of its original formulation. He holds that the question of vicarious atonement must be asked in terms of the relation between the particular and the universal in the humanity of Christ: "How can the restoration of our manhood be brought about by something that happens to the manhood of Jesus?"[25] He steers a middle course between an extreme nominalism, according to which "the name 'man' when applied to different individuals does not signify any kind of sharing in a common essence" and "the opposite extreme of an exaggerated realism

[25] E. L. Mascall, *Christ, the Christian and the Church,* p. 70. Longmans, 1946.

which would make the individuality of the multiplicity of human beings a mere illusion and would attribute reality only to a universal manhood laid up in some sort of Platonic heaven," and he favors a moderate realism (*universalia in re*), according to which "the universal is concretely embodied in the particular manifestations and . . . the only existence that it has antecedently to them is its existence as an idea in the mind of God." [26] Mascall claims it is only by analogy with this notion, which he admits to be "subtle and precarious," that we can begin to understand the great mystery of Christ as the "universal" man, in whom the re-creation of manhood is complete from the moment of the hypostatic union, yet not in such a way as to bring about the re-creation of all individual men automatically.[27] He elaborates a doctrine by which the benefits realized by Christ as the universal man are communicated to us as individuals by our incorporation into his human nature; and this too, he insists, must be understood in ontological terms. He is critical of the Protestant doctrine of forensic justification, which he charges with a nominalistic denial of the reality of the change wrought in us by Christ; and he contends, much like Osiander, that the righteousness of Christ is imparted, and not merely imputed, to us in justification.[28]

These attempts to resuscitate the incarnational theology of the ancient church – others could be cited [29] – have not, of course, been allowed to pass unchallenged. Reactions have varied from wonderment to incomprehension and forthright opposition. The last was exemplified by Rashdall, who, with reference to Moberly's book, delivered a slashing attack on the doctrine, which he found originally suggested in Irenaeus, and "afterwards much developed and not yet quite extinct among us, that in Jesus the whole of humanity – the universal of humanity – suffered death, the appointed penalty of sin, that

[26] *Op. cit.*, p. 72.
[27] *Op. cit.*, p. 74.
[28] *Op. cit.*, pp. 79 ff.
[29] E.g., W. K. Lowther Clarke, *Divine Humanity* (1936), pp. 174 f. S. P. C. K., London.

therefore every individual man may be said to have suffered it; and that so God, having fulfilled his threat that he who sins shall die, is now free to pardon"; elsewhere he describes it as "the old bastard Platonism which makes the universal 'human nature' into an entity separable from any and all individual men, which can contract and discharge obligations – the obligations of humanity and not of any particular man."[30] Rashdall's attitude illustrates the difficulty that the idea presents wherever the inviolability or inalienability of personal ethical responsibility is made axiomatic. Indeed, it points to the question, which was raised by McLeod Campbell's reviewer, whether this principle is compatible with any kind of mediation whatsoever; Rashdall's own theory of the atonement is of the moralistic, Abelardian type.

A. B. Macaulay took a similar attitude. He described Moberly's statement that in his atoning work Christ was "himself man, himself Humanity,"[31] as "a mystico-metaphysical idea which may pardonably, perhaps, be described as unintelligible, except as an unhappy way of expressing the fact that Christ is the Savior of the world, and that in him faith finds all its needs met."[32] Such language reveals a failure to appreciate Moberly's concern to establish the vicarious character of the work of Christ on an objective basis prior to our personal appropriation of it.[33] The fact that Christ is universal Savior is the ground on which faith rests, but faith does not establish it.

There are others who, although conceding that the idea is difficult or unintelligible to the modern mind, do not dismiss it on that account but recognize it as an attempt to express an

[30] H. Rashdall, *The Idea of Atonement in Christian Theology*, pp. 238 and 353. The Macmillan Company, 1919. Cf. p. 424 (note) and Rashdall's essay on Moberly's book in *Journal of Theological Studies*, III, pp. 178–211.

[31] Moberly, *op. cit.*, p. 129.

[32] A. B. Macaulay, *The Death of Jesus*, p. 140. Hodder & Stoughton, Ltd., London, 1938.

[33] Cf. Barth, *KD*, IV, 1, p. 252.

element of the truth that is inexpressible. Nathaniel Micklem has written of it: "This is not a formal theological doctrine; it is an aspect of the mystery of our redemption which is suggested to us by certain passages in Scripture and by a consideration of the teaching of the early fathers of the church. It is not 'orthodox' or 'heretical'; it is a glimpse into the dazzling brightness of the grace of God." [34]

Mascall's book illustrates the difficulties that confront any attempt to rehabilitate the doctrine. The major difficulty resides in the theory of universals on which it rests, and to which reference has already been made. But even if Mascall's brand of moderate realism were accepted, it is doubtful if this can really be used to support the distinctive Christological position, which is expressed in the doctrine of the second Adam, or the archetype (Schleiermacher), viz., that the universal of mankind is embodied in the particular person of Christ in a unique and unparalleled sense. And, finally, there is the difficulty of translating this Christology into other than ontological terms. Mascall is no doubt correct in his view that the terms of the classical Christology are ontological in character and that confusion results if they are taken in a psychological sense. But a Christology that must be strictly confined to ontological terms would surely be docetic. If Christ is true and complete man, it must be possible to raise the question of his person in terms of psychology and ethics, however difficult it may be to find the answers; for it is of the essence of manhood that it is susceptible to ethical and psychological interpretation. The doctrine of the incarnation means that, without prejudice to the uniqueness of Christ, his human nature and human experience are open to the same modes of observation as those of other men. The humanity of Christ must be humanly interpreted, as the means by which God chose to deal with us humanly at the human level.

[34] N. Micklem, *The Doctrine of Our Redemption,* p. 39. Eyre and Spottiswoode, London, 1943.

CHAPTER

VI

The Incarnate Life

THE FREQUENCY with which those who have been concerned with the quest for an adequate ground for the vicarious principle in the atonement have been driven back upon the theology of the incarnation, and the difficulty of making the categories of the classical Christology meaningful to the modern mind, would seem to point to an impasse. Is there any way out? Apparently not, if the Definition of Chalcedon is held to be "complete in theory and legally binding on all later ages,"[1] and the church is committed to literal fidelity to it. This would seem to be the position of the Church of Rome, as it was expressed in the papal encyclical marking the fifteen hundredth anniversary of the council: "No one, enticed by the aberrations of human philosophy or deceived by the tortuosity of human language, dare shake with doubt or pervert with harmful innovations the dogma defined at Chalcedon, that in Christ there are two true and perfect natures, one divine and one human, joined together but not confused, and subsisting in the sole Person of the Word."[2] And, of course, there are others, in the Church of England and elsewhere, who take much the same position. But within the last century or so there has also been a succession of theologians, who, although not unsympathetic to the general intention of the Chalcedonian

[1] H. R. Mackintosh, *The Person of Christ*, p. 292. T. & T. Clark, 1912.

[2] *Sempiternus Rex*, September 8, 1951 (quoted from *The New York Times* of September 13, 1951).

Definition, have questioned the propriety or the adequacy of the terms in which it is formulated. In particular, the use of the concept " nature " in the statement of the person of Christ has been the object of a persistent strain of criticism. An early critic was Schleiermacher, who voiced two objections to it. The first is interesting because it anticipates Barth's objection to the Catholic doctrine of *analogia entis;* he asked, " How can divine and human be thus brought together under any single conception, as if they could both be more exact determinations, co-ordinated to each other, of one and the same universal? "[3] His second objection to it was that in modern speech it connotes the realm of the physical as distinct from the historical. Schleiermacher was aware that the term did not bear this narrow connotation in the ancient church and that it was employed in a comprehensive sense for the being of man (as also of God) in its unity and totality.[4] Nevertheless the feeling that the term has preponderantly physical associations persisted, and the objection to its use on this score was renewed with special vehemence in the Ritschlian School on the ground that it was bound up with a physical theory of salvation that was incompatible with the ethical character of Christianity. This view was widely shared in the latter part of the nineteenth century and the early years of the twentieth and found frequent expression in the English-speaking world. To H. R. Mackintosh the term " nature " was, among other things, " insufficiently ethical "; [5] and he refers to P. T. Forsyth as one who " has shown us that the moralizing of dogma is an essential of all modern Christian thought."[6]

Now this plea for ethical categories in the restatement of Christology has for us almost as one-sided a sound as the category of nature to which objection was made. If the two-natures

[3] *The Christian Faith,* § 96, 1 (ET, p. 392).
[4] Cf. Barth, *KD,* I, 2, pp. 140 f.
[5] Mackintosh, *op. cit.,* p. 294.
[6] *Op. cit.,* p. 302.

Christology was bound up with a quasi-physical theory of salvation, the proposed ethical restatement would seem to point to a Pelagian and even a humanistic version of Christianity. But this was far from being the case, at any rate with the two theologians who have been named as representative of the Christological thought of the period. Their use of the term "ethical" is somewhat misleading; neither Forsyth nor Mackintosh was thinking of a reduction of the fact of Christ to ethical terms in the strict sense of the word; both were using it in a broad sense to indicate an approach to the Christological problem that was made, not merely from the standpoint of the ontological constitution of the Person of Christ in the traditional sense, but from a perspective that embraced the *entire* fact of Christ, his incarnate life and work, his death and resurrection, and not merely his *assumptio carnis*. It may be granted that both tended to view the entire fact in a predominantly ethical light, but their real intention in using the term "ethical" (for want of a better) was to protest against the preoccupation of Christological thought with one aspect of the fact of Christ, which they considered to be devoid of ethical significance, and to point to the relevance for Christology of his historical life and ministry. The influence of "the rediscovery of the Jesus of history" is clearly in evidence here; but the plea was not merely for a reconsideration of the work of Christ; it was for a consideration of the bearing of the rediscovered Jesus of history on the Christological problem as such. Mackintosh expressed the view that some of the persistent difficulties of Christology were due to the narrow perspective from which they had been approached and that a broadening of the perspective to include the Jesus of history might relieve them. It was with this in mind that he pleaded for a "restatement of Christology in personal and spiritual terms."[7] One approach to the desired restatement of Christology, which was favored by Mackintosh and several others about this time, was by way

[7] *Op. cit.*, p. 303.

of revision of the accepted connotation of the term "incarnation." It had long been assumed in theological discourse that the incarnation refers to the act of Christ's taking our nature upon him (*assumptio carnis*) and thus relates in a special sense to the Nativity. The assumption underlies the traditional division of the doctrine of the person of Christ from that of his work and of his status, and implies that the question of the person of Christ can be isolated and intelligibly considered by itself. Growing dissatisfaction with this compartmentalization of the fact of Christ, which, though academically convenient, was felt to be artificial and misleading, led to a questioning of the assumption that underlies it. When the New Testament declares that the Word was made flesh and dwelt among us, is it referring to the incarnation in the formal sense, the *assumptio carnis* by the eternal Logos, the hypostatic union of the Chalcedonian Definition? The answer that Denney gave to this question in characteristically incisive terms was indicative of the new approach: "The only incarnation of which the New Testament knows anything is the appearance of Christ in the race and lot of sinful men, and his endurance in it to the end. Apart from sharing our experience, that sharing of our nature, which is sometimes supposed to be what is meant by incarnation, is an abstraction and a figment."[8] If the incarnation be viewed in this way as coextensive with the whole life and ministry of Christ and not merely as his entrance upon it at the Nativity, this means, as Denney's words suggest, that when we seek to interpret it we must use categories of history and experience and not merely those of nature. The criticism frequently brought against the traditional doctrine was that its categories were altogether too static.[9] As P. T. Forsyth put it, they were framed "at a time when the theology of redemption

[8] Denney, *The Christian Doctrine of Reconciliation*, p. 242. Cf. pp. 183 f. Doran, 1918.

[9] Mackintosh, *op. cit.*, pp. 491 ff.; L. Hodgson, *Christian Faith and Practice*, p. 68, Blackwell, 1950; D. D. Williams, *What Present-Day Theologians Are Thinking*, pp. 102 f., Harper & Brothers, 1952.

was apt to be conceived in terms of substance rather than subject, of metaphysic rather than ethic, of things rather than persons. . . . But we have come to a time in the growth of Christian moral culture when personal relations and personal movements count for more than the relations of the most rare and ethereal substances," and, therefore, he continued, we must seek to understand the person of Christ in terms of "a metaphysic of history and not of being, of soul and not of substance, of the moral soul and not the noetic substance, of ethic and not of thoughts." [10]

The outcome of the application of these dynamic categories to the problem was the proposal to interpret the incarnation as a developing process which continued over a period and advanced to a consummation. The first to put forward the conception, which came to be known as gradual, or progressive incarnation, was the German theologian, Isaak August Dorner, who argued that since growth is an essential element in human life, a place must be given in Christology to the human growth of Christ, and if this is done, it follows that "with the growth of the human side there is also necessarily given in him a growth of the God-humanity; and the incarnation is not to be thought of as at once completed, but as continuous, nay, augmentative, seeing that God as Logos ever seizes and appropriates those of the new sides which are generated by the true human development." [11] The prestige that the whole idea of development had acquired at the time lent some attraction to the conception, in addition to the fact that it found a Christological significance in the historical life of Christ. The fact that the church adheres to the exalted Christ, said Dorner, does not mean that his temporal life is of secondary importance. He found a deeper wisdom in the church's liturgy than its theology here; he recalled that "the church in its annual

[10] P. T. Forsyth, *The Person and Place of Jesus Christ,* pp. 331 f. Hodder & Stoughton, 1911.

[11] I. A. Dorner, *System of Christian Doctrine,* III, p. 328. T. & T. Clark, 1885.

cycle of feasts lives through the life of Christ again from the manger to the ascension," and he maintained that "Christ's earthly life is not incidental; the knowledge of it is the only right way leading to the knowledge of the exalted Christ."[12] The idea of a progressive incarnation was taken up by Forsyth and Mackintosh. Forsyth sought to present it as the embodiment in Christ of "the two movements of spiritual reality in which man and God meet,"[13] and he followed Dorner closely in holding that the moral growth, which is essential to true humanity, meant "the growing appropriation of Jesus of his divine content as he becomes a fuller organ for God's full action on man."[14] In a similar way Mackintosh insisted on allowing a place to growth in the humanity of Christ, and since growth cannot be predicated of the part and not of the whole, he drew the conclusion that "the union of God and man in him was more completely actualized at death than at birth, when he rose than when he died."[15]

The idea of progressive incarnation presents difficulties. The type of question most frequently raised regarding it is this: If the union of God and man was a process, are we to think of the God-manhood as a result that was realized at the completion of the process, and not beforehand? The defenders of the idea have usually replied that the growth of Christ was growth *in* God-manhood rather than growth *to* God-manhood; it was to be viewed, not as a movement from desire to fulfillment, or from imperfection to perfection, but rather as a movement from potentiality to actuality.[16] The union of divine and human was present in Christ from the beginning; only, since the capacities of humanity, such as consciousness, are latent at the beginning, the union could not be realized in them until they

[12] Dorner, *op. cit.*, p. 329.
[13] Forsyth, *op. cit.*, p. 339.
[14] *Op. cit.*, p. 344.
[15] Mackintosh, *op. cit.*, p. 495.
[16] Cf. Mackintosh, *op. cit.*, pp. 496 ff.; Forsyth, *op. cit.*, p. 342.

developed.[17] If this answer is not fully convincing, it may be because the question itself presupposes the standpoint of the traditional doctrine with its static categories; if the incarnation is in fact a process, then to ask whether it exists or not at some specified point in the process is to repeat the ancient absurdity of Achilles and the tortoise. The question did indeed appear to be legitimated by the designation of the new conception as gradual or progressive incarnation; for this phrase could suggest a view of the incarnation as a result achieved by a gradual process, and then it would be important to determine the precise point at which the result was achieved.[18] But none of those who used the phrase intended it to be interpreted in this sense (although Dorner was thought to do so). Their intention was to present a view of the incarnation as having its reality in the process as a whole; they saw it as essentially a dynamic reality which could only be interpreted in the dynamic category of *genesis* (becoming) and which the static category of *physis,* employed by the ancient church, could not grasp without distortion.

Notable support for this view has come lately from Karl Barth. Barth rejects the traditional division between the doctrines of the person and the work of Christ, although he concedes its usefulness for purposes of teaching, on the ground that it implies that the question, Who Christ is, can be answered in abstraction from the question, What he does. The two, he contends, cannot be separated. Christ is presented in the New Testament as the subject of a certain activity; his being is in the concrete events of a history. Barth holds that the dogmatic definitions of Nicaea, Chalcedon, etc., although they ostensibly deal with "the being of Christ," were intended as guiding lines for the understanding of "his existence and ac-

[17] Cf. Dorner, *op. cit.*, III, pp. 335 f.

[18] It is sometimes necessary for legal purposes to define one precise moment in the *process* of birth at which a child can be held to be born, but it can only be done in an arbitrary way.

tion," and not as "building materials for the construction of an abstract doctrine of his person."[19] In his own existential[20] treatment of the doctrine he brings the person of Christ into integral relationship with his work, and more particularly, he seeks to combine in a novel and interesting manner the doctrine of the two "natures," the divine and the human, with the doctrine of the two "states" of humiliation and exaltation, each of which, he maintains, must be interpreted in the light of the other. Humiliation and exaltation are not to be regarded as two successive stages in the history of Jesus Christ but as two sides of the one work of reconciliation which filled his whole existence; they represent "the *actuality* of the being of Jesus Christ as true God and true man."[21] And so the divinity of Jesus Christ is not to be defined in terms of an abstract (and *a priori*) conception of divine "nature" but in terms of the dynamic concept of humiliation, and his humanity likewise in terms of exaltation.

Barth claims for this method of approach that, without being untrue to the classical Christology, it corresponds much more closely to the testimony of the New Testament, which, while it is full of Christology, never sets up a doctrine of the person of Christ in abstraction from his work. Those who recognize Barth's claim will view his attempt at integration with sympathy, even though they may not be able to assent to every detail in its execution. However, it is not our present purpose to pursue the development of this "actualistic" approach to the Christological problem as such, but rather to confine ourselves to that specific aspect of the problem which we have singled out for attention, viz., the relation between the humanity of Christ and ours, which forms the basis of his vicarious work. The question is: Can the truth that the classical Christology sought to express in terms of abstract essence be more adequately expressed in terms of the history of the

19 Barth, *KD*, IV, 1, pp. 135 ff.

20 The term is mine, not Barth's.

21 *KD*, IV, 1, p. 146.

incarnate life? Can we perhaps say that the "universal manhood" is the real meaning of "the Jesus of history"?

When we read the Gospels with this question in mind, there are certain features of the life they record which immediately appear in a suggestive light.

1. The first is very general. If we survey the human life of Christ as a whole, what is the chief characteristic it exhibits? Undoubtedly, it is what we may call – to adapt one of Riesman's terms – its other-centeredness. This life is other-centered, and that, uniquely, in a double sense. The life of Christ is wholly centered upon God. As Moberly put it, "The center of his life is never in himself. He is always, explicitly, the manifestation, the reflection, the obedient son and servant, of another. There is no purpose of self; no element of self-will; no possibility, even for a moment, of the imagination of separateness."[22] The concentration of Christ's whole existence upon God is frequently expressed in the Fourth Gospel: "I can of myself do nothing: as I hear, I judge: and my judgment is righteous; because I seek not mine own will, but the will of him that sent me" (John 5:30); and "The words that I say unto you I speak not from myself: but the Father abiding in me doeth his works" (John 14:10). All these phrases, says Moberly, reiterate "the central truth, that the focus or center of his being as man, was not in himself as man, but in his Father, that is God."[23] The Son is the authentic expression of the Father's mind and will, because there exists between him and the Father a relation of mutual indwelling: "I am in the Father, and the Father in me" (John 14:10). It is a relation that may be remotely compared with that of two concentric circles. All the life of Christ radiates from that center where he is one with the Father. And in like manner it is all directed toward that center. It has a double movement, centrifugal and centripetal, because it is governed by the double fact that

[22] *Atonement and Personality*, p. 99.

[23] *Op. cit.*, p. 104.

"he was come from God, and went to God" (John 13:3).

But there is another side to the picture. While the life of Christ is wholly centered on God, it is at the same time wholly open to men. Barth has expressed this dual characteristic of the life of Christ in two simple, but eloquent phrases: "He is the man for God, and he is the man for other men." [24] The two things do not naturally go together; on the contrary, they tend to be antithetical. A life so God-centered as Jesus' was tends to isolate a man and set him apart from his fellows, whereas those most open to their fellow men do not always walk with God. In Jesus neither relationship is sacrificed to the other; both are present in him and interpenetrate each other in a unique way. Both McLeod Campbell and Barth have pointed out that Christ's so-called summary of the law in the two commandments of love is the law of his own life, in which it is perfectly manifested. "The structure of the humanity of Jesus himself which is disclosed in this twofold commandment," [25] is that in him "the spirit of Sonship, in which consists the perfect fulfillment of the first commandment, is one with the spirit of brotherhood which is the fulfillment of the second. Loving the Father with all his heart and mind and soul and strength, the Savior loved his brethren as himself." [26] The two relationships are integrally bound together in him. This does not mean that they coincide with each other,[27] or that both are equally actual at every moment of his existence. Barth has said, in another notable phrase, that "the manhood of Jesus may be unequivocally described as fellow-manhood"; [28] but when he goes on to expound this to mean that in Jesus there was "nothing like an inmost, deepest recess where he was for himself or for God alone, where he enjoyed an existence of

[24] *KD,* III, 2, § 44, 1, and § 45, 1.
[25] Barth, *KD,* III, 2, p. 258.
[26] Campbell, *The Nature of the Atonement,* p. 108.
[27] The second commandment of love is *like* the first, not identical with it (Mark 12:31).
[28] *KD,* III, 2, p. 248.

stoic detachment or mystical rapture apart from his fellow men and unaffected by their condition and fate,"[29] we may question whether this is quite the picture presented by the Gospels. It would seem rather that in faithfulness to the records we must think of a certain alternation between the two relations. The Gospels record a series of occasions when Jesus "departed" and "withdrew" himself from the society of men — not indeed to seek a stoic or mystical isolation — but in order to be alone with God (Mark 1:35; 6:46; etc.). His life would have been less than truly human had it not obeyed the rhythm of "withdrawal and return,"[30] which belongs to the pattern of human existence. We may surely suppose that Jesus spent more time than the rest of us in prayerful communion with God. Yet this did not make him a solitary; from every period of communion with God he returned to the world of men to enter more deeply into solidarity with them. A whole night in prayer on a mountain is followed by the calling of the disciples (Luke 6:12 ff.); the transfiguration is the prelude to the Passion (Mark 9:2–13); Gethsemane prepares the way for Calvary (Mark 14:41). Each withdrawal on the part of Jesus is a *reculer pour mieux sauter,* a preparation for a closer and deeper identification of himself with men. The life of Jesus was essentially a public life, a life that was (literally) spent for others.

This relation to others in which Jesus spent his life we call love, *agape,* love that gives; but the term has worn somewhat thin through constant usage, and it is worth-while to recall another term in which it is more specifically defined in the Synoptics. Barth has drawn attention to the peculiar manner in which the verb *splagchnizesthai* is applied to Jesus in the Gospels. The word, derived from *splagchna,* "the nobler viscera," denotes an emotion that penetrates to the inmost depths of one's being, and for which "to have mercy" or "compassion" is too

[29] *Op. cit.,* pp. 251 f.
[30] The phrase is borrowed from Toynbee, *A Study of History* (abridgment), pp. 217–222. Oxford University Press, 1947.

weak a rendering. When applied to Jesus, it means, in Barth's words, that " the pain, the sin, the absolutely forlorn and desperate condition of these men and this people not only affected Jesus, not only touched his heart, but so entered into his heart, into his very self, that all this misery was now in him and became his own misery, and as such was much more acutely realized and more painfully felt by him than by them; *esplagchnisthei* means: he took this misery upon himself, he took it away from them and made it his own affair, his own misery." [31] A conspicuous feature of the Gospel narratives is is that wherever he went, his presence acted as a magnet for the sick, the halt, the maimed, and the blind. Men felt that here was something more than sympathy; here was such a drawing of their need into his inmost being that it could only be described in the words of ancient prophecy: " Himself took our infirmities, and bare our sicknesses " (Matt. 8:17).

The compassion of Jesus for human need, while it has never gone wholly unrecognized, has made an especially powerful appeal to modern humanitarian feeling; and among the theologians who have been engaged in the application of Forsyth's program for " the moralizing of dogma " to the problem of the atonement, there are several who have found in it a useful and important clue. Is it not, indeed, almost self-evident that if we are seeking to know how Jesus died for men, we should begin by looking at how he lived for them? How can we hope to understand the death of Jesus except in the light of the life that it consummated?

Those who have taken this approach to the problem have pointed to the unitive power of love in human relations and have sought in it a basis for the vicarious principle in atonement. Love is a personal relationship; it presupposes the distinctness of the persons concerned; but it is the very nature of love to transcend the boundaries of personal distinctness and to weld the persons together in a unity in which it is the most

[31] *KD*, III, 2, p. 252.

natural thing for one to act vicariously for another. The principle of vicarious action, it is held, and still more that of vicarious passion, "is written large on the face of all life."[32] It is manifested in the willing endurance of suffering by a mother for her child, or by a soldier for his country, and in the sacrifice a man will make for his friend. This principle, it has been said, is "no far-off theological mystery, but . . . the very texture of our human experience."[33] And the vicarious death of Christ is but the supreme instance of it. There is no need to refer it to an arbitrary and inscrutable divine appointment; it has its sufficient basis in the love in which he identified himself with men. "There is something," writes McLeod Campbell, "which surely commends itself to us in this recognition of love as that which identifies the Savior with those to whom he is a Savior."[34] It was a central element in the thought of Horace Bushnell that "Love is a principle essentially vicarious in its own nature, identifying the subject with others, so as to suffer their adversities and pains, and taking on itself the burden of their evils. . . . This is the true law of interpretation, when the vicarious relation of Christ to our sins comes into view."[35] It is admitted that the relation of Christ to sinful men, which is implied in the doctrine of the atonement, goes far beyond anything that is found in ordinary human experience, but not so far as to be completely incomprehensible. "Human analogies," writes Vincent Taylor, "help us up to a point, but it is no matter for wonder if they do not take us all the way,"[36] and he cites Paul Althaus' words: "How are we, who as sinners cannot know what perfect love is, to understand what complete solidarity may be achieved by perfect love?"[37]

A more recent phase of philosophic reflection has gone on

[32] T. Hywel Hughes, *The Atonement,* p. 134.
[33] A. S. Pringle-Pattison, *The Idea of God,* p. 417.
[34] *Op. cit.,* p. 108.
[35] *The Vicarious Sacrifice,* p. 7. Charles Scribner's Sons, 1877.
[36] *Jesus and His Sacrifice,* p. 312. The Macmillan Company, 1937.
[37] *Mysterium Christi,* p. 210. Longmans, 1930.

to maintain that this principle belongs to the very structure of personal being. Personal being is essentially being in relation, not being in isolation. The first personal pronoun has been removed from that lonely eminence it has occupied in the thinking of philosophers since Descartes, and the second has now taken its place alongside it. The pattern of personal being is no longer conceived as a circle with " I " at the center; it has become an ellipse with two foci, " I and Thou." It is, of course, in Martin Buber's book of that title that this insight received its classical formulation (although there were others who preceived it and expressed it in their own ways long before Buber),[38] and it has been taken up by many others, such as Ferdinand Ebner,[39] Emil Brunner,[40] and finally even by Karl Barth (who formerly " persecuted this way ").[41] In all of these we find the contention, variously expressed, that the fundamental form of human existence is not individual isolation, but " togetherness "; there can be no I without a Thou; they exist in mutual interdependence; all real life is meeting; to be a person means to be in relation to other persons. This conception of personal being does not obliterate the frontiers of individual selfhood; for there can be no relation to others with-

[38] To name only a few, H. R. Mackintosh, *op. cit.*, pp. 338 f.; W. Temple, *The Nature of Personality;* R. C. Moberly, who made it one of the main themes of his great book *Atonement and Personality*, that the essence of personality is not mutual exclusiveness or mutual impenetrability; and above all, Dostoevsky; cf. *The Brothers Karamazov*, Book VI, Ch. II, " The Recollections of Father Zossima." Of course, Buber's treatment is highly original, but his central theme is " What oft was thought but ne'er so well expressed." Parallel to this development, and perhaps related to it, there has been a revival of interest in the Biblical idea of " corporate personality "; cf. H. Wheeler Robinson, *Redemption and Revelation*, pp. 246 ff., James Nisbet & Co., Ltd., London, 1942.

[39] *Das Wort und die geistigen Realitäten.*

[40] *Man in Revolt.* The Westminster Press, 1939.

[41] *KD*, III, 2, § 45, 2. For Barth's earlier view, see his article " *Das erste Gebot als theologisches Axiom* " in *Zwischen den Zeiten*, 1933, p. 311; and compare Brunner's article on " The New Barth " in *Scottish Journal of Theology* IV (1951), p. 127.

out distinction from others; as Barth says, "When I utter the word 'I,' I effect a distinction and at the same time a relation."[42] But it enables us to see that individual selves are not so imprisoned behind these frontiers as to be impenetrable to others.

Now it is obvious that the problem of vicarious atonement becomes less intractable when it is viewed in the light of this conception of personality rather than that of the older "adamantine theory," as it has been called. This was the thesis of Moberly's book. But it is also obvious that there is a danger of overshooting the mark; for if the revised conception of personality serves to "explain" the mystery of atonement, it would seem to be at the risk of explaining it away, if the effect is "to suggest that it is only an extension of principles already implicit in our social existence as human beings when we speak of a true solidarity of life, a spiritual coalescence, between Christ and his people."[43] Is not the uniqueness of Christ imperiled if his relation to men, which underlies his vicarious work, rests on a principle that is universally present in humanity? It may be said in reply that, if the humanity of Christ, together with what it implies for his relation to his fellow men, is truly consubstantial with ours and like it in all respects, except for sin, it falls into the general category of humanity and may legitimately be interpreted in the light of the humanity of other men; so that when the fathers at Chalcedon declared Christ to be consubstantial with us as regards the manhood, they meant that he is related to us in precisely the same way as we are all related to one another. On this view, then, the uniqueness of Christ resides exclusively in his divinity, and not at all in his humanity. Were the relation of Christ to mankind to be grounded in his humanity, it would be limited in extent, as each one of ours is. It is his divinity that gives Christ his universal significance, or, as Du Bose put it, "It is God in it which makes that particular humanity of our Lord . . .

[42] *KD*, III, 2, p. 292. [43] H. R. Mackintosh, *op. cit.*, p. 339.

valid and available for all."[44] This was the view of Aquinas, as we saw, and it has been reaffirmed in our own time by Karl Barth who, despite the large use he makes of the notion of human solidarity, ascribes the substitution of Christ ultimately to his divinity: "It is because he was the Son of God and himself God that he had the competence and the power to suffer in our place."[45] But this kind of appeal to the divinity of Christ savors more than a little of *deus ex machina,* and though the humanity is accorded a subordinate and instrumental role, there seems no compelling reason why it should have even so much if the vicarious power resides ultimately in the divinity. The ancient church saw the basis of Christ's relation to men in his humanity, and though they supported this view with a metaphysical theory that is no longer acceptable, it is a question whether their view was not fundamentally more in harmony with the testimony of the New Testament and with the self-understanding of Jesus.

2. Jesus' chosen self-designation as "Son of Man" seems to point in this direction. The name is, of course, mysterious — perhaps it was intended to be — and its meaning has been much debated;[46] indeed, it has been said that "on no subject in the teaching of Jesus has scholarship been more divided and at a loss."[47] The main difficulty has been to determine the source from which Jesus derived the term. If, however, we discard the assumption, which has underlain much of the debate, that the term must needs bear the same meaning in the mouth of Jesus as it did in the source from which he may be presumed to have taken it, and if we look rather for the mean-

[44] *The Gospel According to St. Paul,* pp. 297 f.

[45] *KD,* IV, 1, p. 244.

[46] Cf. T. W. Manson, *The Teaching of Jesus,* Ch. VIII, Cambridge University Press, 1931; W. A. Curtis, *Jesus Christ, the Teacher,* Oxford University Press, 1943; G. S. Duncan, *Jesus, Son of Man,* Ch. XI, James Nisbet & Co., Ltd., London, 1947; T. W. Manson, *Jesus the Messiah,* pp. 113 ff., Hodder & Stoughton, London, 1943; A. M. Hunter, *The Work and Words of Jesus,* pp. 84 ff., The Westminster Press, 1950.

[47] Curtis, *op. cit.,* p. 135.

ing that Jesus gave it in his own rendering of the role, there are certain things about it that it seems we can set down with some degree of assurance.

a. Jesus' predilection for this name, contrasted with his marked reluctance to accept the title of Messiah, weighs heavily against the view that the "Son of Man" is simply a synonym for Messiah and carries with it the apocalyptic associations that it bears in the books of Daniel and Enoch. There seems to be more truth in the view that Jesus' use of the name has a close affinity with that of Ezekiel.[48]

b. The use of "Son of Man" in the Old Testament as a generic term for man (e.g., Ps. 8:4) would appear to lend it a more than individual significance. And its use in Dan. 7:13 ff., which many regard as the source from which Jesus derived the term, also points in this direction; for the visionary figure of "one like to a son of man," who appears in contrast to the four beasts, is interpreted as representing "the saints of the Most High." Thus, while Jesus used the name with reference to himself individually, almost as a synonym for the first personal pronoun, "it seems a reasonable presupposition," as Duncan says, "that in some way which calls for fuller examination he intended it to express his relationship to the 'sons of men.' There was some sense in which he regarded himself as 'the man'—a unique and true representative of his brethren of mankind, fully at one with them, while in some way also distinct from them."[49] The Son of Man is a unique figure, but his uniqueness lies in his devoting himself "for us" and being "the man for other men."

c. Even if "Son of Man" is a Messianic title, Jesus' choice of this title in preference to all others surely indicates that he conceived his Messianic mission as one to be fulfilled in terms of human action. It used to be thought that Jesus' use of the name was only his way of asserting his true humanity in the

[48] Curtis, *op. cit.*, pp. 138 ff.; Duncan, *op. cit.*, p. 146.
[49] Duncan, *op. cit.*, p. 136.

Christological sense, and, though modern research has shown this view to be much too simple, it ought not to be allowed to blind us to the element of truth contained in it. Whoever the Son of Man may denote, the name connotes a human figure, one who accomplishes his mission in essentially human terms. And if the mission of the Son of Man is vicarious, it would seem too that his vicarious relation to others is to be established humanly, through human action and interaction, rather than by some unaccountable exercise of divine power. It is surely significant that in some of the most solemn statements concerning the vicarious scope of his mission, Jesus speaks of himself as the Son of Man; it is the Son of Man who must suffer (Mark 8:31), because it is the mission of the Son of Man to serve others and to spend his life for them (Mark 10:45).

3. The vicarious relation of Christ to men has sometimes been described as an exchange; [50] Luther was fond of putting it this way,[51] and Barth has recently declared that it is impossible to describe what really took place in Christ without using the term.[52] "For our sake he made him to be sin who knew no sin, so that in him we might become the righteousness of God." (II Cor. 5:21.) Does the conception not become more intelligible and more convincing to us if we look at this exchange as something accomplished by Christ in the whole course of his incarnate life rather than as something established by his birth alone or his death alone? There are certain elements in the recorded life that lend support to such a view:

a. The baptism of Jesus would seem to mark the beginning of the exchange, his formal entry upon the mission of being "the man for other men." It is well known that the baptism has long presented a difficult exegetical problem, but there appears

[50] The earliest instance is in the *Epistle to Diognetus,* Ch. 9.
[51] Cf. his *Commentary on Galatians* 3:13.
[52] *KD,* IV, 1, pp. 79 ff.; cf. pp. 261 ff.

to be a growing consensus among modern commentators that in some way it signifies Jesus' association of himself with his brethren of mankind in their deepest need. Indeed, it is hard to interpret it in any other way. If Jesus had no sins of his own to repent of, what need had he to be baptized? Matthew relates that when Jesus came to be baptized, "John forbade him, saying, I have need to be baptized of thee, and comest thou to me?" (Matt. 3:14). By all normal standards Jesus ought to have been the baptizer, not the baptized. But here we have something that goes beyond "the lore of nicely calculated less or more"; here we have the first glimpse of the mystery of Jesus' "entry into solidarity with our need and fellowship with our lost existence,"[53] which was to be consummated (Luke 12:50) in his laying down his life for us on the cross. "It was," wrote A. B. Macaulay, "an act inspired by a vicarious impulse of love, the act of the Suffering Servant 'numbering himself with the transgressors,' an identification of himself with them in their relation to God as sinners, a taking upon himself of the burden of their redemption with all that he foresaw was involved in such a work."[54] If this is true – and it can hardly be otherwise – then we should be able to read the subsequent history of the life of Jesus as the record of the fulfillment of his baptismal vow by the consolidation of this unique relationship to men, until it was perfected when he died, as Athanasius put it,[55] with his arms outstretched to embrace all mankind.

b. A quite superficial survey of the relations of Jesus to men throughout the course of his public ministry reveals a significant fluctuation. Broadly speaking, the public ministry of Jesus falls into two divisions. The first is characterized by a general acceptance of Jesus by the people; the second, in a more decided way, by his rejection. In the first period, which is roughly that of the Galilean ministry, the characteristic

[53] *KD,* I, 2, p. 167.
[54] *The Death of Jesus,* p. 95.
[55] *On the Incarnation,* Ch. 25.

picture is one of Jesus surrounded by crowds welcoming him wherever he goes, hanging on his words and eagerly expectant of his deeds. But there comes a point, well marked by all the Evangelists (cf. Mark 10:32; Luke 9:51–62; and especially John 6:66–71) – roughly the point of his turning from Galilee to Jerusalem – when the picture dramatically changes: the crowds drift away, and Jesus is left more or less with the Twelve; and then at the final crisis they all forsook him and fled, and he died on the cross alone. If the relation between Jesus and men is measured in terms of popular acceptance, it would have to be represented on a graph by a descending line. But to view it only in this way would be to miss the wonder of it; for the wonder of it is that when we consider the relationship more inwardly from the angle of Jesus himself, it appears as an ascending line which intersects the other in a paradoxical way. The people's acceptance and rejection of Jesus do not correspond to acceptance and rejection of them on his part. On the contrary, we seem to see here an aspect of the "exchange" in operation. During the period of the people's acceptance of him Jesus appears in some ways to be bent on rejecting them; he comes on the scene as the messenger of judgment, proclaiming the Kingdom of God and his righteousness and sounding the call to repentance. In the Sermon on the Mount he sets forth the new law with its lofty requirements which no one can ever hope to observe; he presents the terms of discipleship in the most stringent and uncompromising form; he subjects the motives of men to merciless analysis. In all, he presents such a challenging attitude to men that he seems to be deliberately alienating them and severing himself from them. Then comes the second period, and his attitude appears to undergo a change. It is almost as if having procured of the people their rejection of him, he exchanges it for his acceptance of them. It is now that he enters definitively on the role of the Suffering Servant, the Son of Man, whose mission and destiny it is to be "the man for other men." The more they are against him, the more he is for them. The more they reject him, the more he accepts them. The more they drive him from them, the more he draws them to him. And the moment of their utmost hostility is the moment of his supreme self-identification with them. The death with which they thought to carry out their "Away with him" is the crown and consummation of his life for them. His execution at their hands is their expiation at his.

Karl Barth notes the sequence of these contrasted phases in the life of Jesus and sees in it that exchange of responsibility for sin which is central to the "penal-substitutionary" view of the atonement. According to him, the characteristic of the first phase is that Jesus comes as the herald of judgment to Israel and the whole world of men; he appears in the role sketched for him by John the Baptist and plays a supremely active part. The second phase we should expect to usher in the fulfillment of this judgment, and in a way it does so – only, the judgment falls, not upon guilty Israel and the world, but upon the one innocent man in their midst; the judge himself steps into the place of the judged and assumes the responsibility for their sin. Christ passes from action to passion.[56]

Although we are grateful to Barth for seeking the exchange in the evangelical history of the life of Christ, there are two objections to the interpretation that he lays upon it: The first is that there is no firm support in the recorded words of Jesus himself for the view that he took upon himself the responsibility for the sins of men. Jesus may well be said to exchange the role of the judge for that of the judged, but there is no word of his to suggest that the judgment he bore is the judgment he brought, i.e., that he deliberately submitted himself to the judgment of God on human sin. The second objection concerns the view of the atonement with which Barth's interpretation is connected. The doctrine of the atonement will be considered more fully in the next chapter, but it may be

[56] *KD,* IV, 1, pp. 246 ff.

sufficient to say here that the view, or type of view, to which Barth subscribes, is grounded on the principle that the judgment of sin must be executed one way or another before sin can be "put away." It would seem to follow that there can be no "remission" of sin prior to the actual execution of the judgment and also that there be no need for it afterward. But both these consequences conflict with the Gospel record. Jesus dispensed the forgiveness of God right from the outset of his ministry, and indeed it was his claim to possess this authority, rather than his proclamation of judgment, that brought him into collision with the official representatives of the Jewish religion.[57] And by the same token the note of judgment continues to sound to the end of the earthly ministry of Jesus, and it forms the keynote of its eschatological consummation; the return of the Son of Man is emphatically a return to judgment (cf. Matt. 16:27; 25:31).

So, even if it remains true that what took place in the course of the incarnate life of Christ may be not inaptly described as an exchange, it is doubtful if we can go so far as to call it an exchange of responsibility for sin between the guilty and the innocent and a consequent exchange of judgment for forgiveness. It is an exchange between unrelieved liability on the part of men to the judgment of God and access to the forgiveness of God through the man in whom it is personally present. The Son of Man comes as the herald of the rule of God in which the judgment of God on the sin of men is effected in its most drastic form — by forgiveness. The Son of Man comes as the bearer of this forgiveness; he comes to dispense it to men by relating himself to them, by being "the man for other men." And it is theirs as they receive it at his hands, by becoming related to him. He is the Man for God who claims men completely for God, and he is the Son of Man who imparts God

[57] Mark 2:1–12. It should be noted that the "blasphemy" of Jesus in the eyes of the scribes did not consist in his assuming that God is free to forgive, for they too took this for granted; it was his assumption of the authority to exercise this divine prerogative.

completely to men. He is the nucleus or center through whom both the inexorable demands of the righteousness of God and the inexpressible grace of his forgiveness are disseminated through mankind. It was to be this center of humanity that he became incarnate as the Son of Man. He formally entered upon it at his baptism, and at his death he carried it to its consummation when he gave himself for us and said *tetelestai,* "It is finished" (John 19:30): The incarnation of the Son of Man was complete.

CHAPTER

VII

The Living of Forgiveness

It is the main thesis of this study that the Christian gospel, which is for our salvation, resides in the total fact of Christ, and that it is inevitably distorted if it is made to hinge in an exclusive manner on one element, such as his birth or his death. In particular, the endeavor has been to show that the vicarious nature of the work of Christ is best understood if its ground is sought in the evangelical record of his incarnate life; in other words, that neither his death for us nor his birth for us can be separated from his whole being for us. It is appropriate now to consider the question of the atonement in the light of this comprehensive perspective.

The central question to which the answer has been sought in discussions of the atonement is, What did Christ do to accomplish our salvation? The answers that have been offered to this question are astonishingly numerous and varied, and it is manifestly impossible to examine them all here. There is, however, one aspect of the question that, if isolated, can provide the basis for a simple classification.[1] If we ask, *To whom* did Christ do what he did, and toward whom was it directed, we find that the answers which have been given fall into three groups.

First, in order of chronology, is the theory, held widely and indeed almost universally until the time of Anselm, that the work of Christ consisted of a victorious conflict with the powers of evil. In this theory, which Aulén has called the

[1] Cf. J. K. Mozley, *The Doctrine of the Atonement*, p. 173.

classic theory,[2] Christ, the God-man, came to act upon the enemy of God and man, that is, the devil. The second type is represented by the theory of Anselm and followed by the Reformers and the majority of modern writers on the subject: here it is God toward whom the atoning work of Christ is directed. Christ is held to have done something to God — either he discharged a debt or he paid a penalty or he performed an act of obedience or he made a confession or he offered a sacrifice — by means of which he procured forgiveness for man. These theories are sometimes classified as transactional, because they make forgiveness the outcome of a transaction between the Son and the Father. The third type is associated with the name of Abelard and is sometimes labeled subjective. Here the work of Christ is directed toward man; he saves us by the moral influence that he exerts upon us as our example.

The Abelardian theory has never enjoyed the support of more than a small minority — although that minority has included some eminent names. Most of his critics have admitted the truth for which Abelard contended, viz., that Christ exercises a moral influence upon men by the example of his patient love and endurance, but have disputed its adequacy; for if this were the whole truth, it would reduce the work of Christ to a demonstration, and as Harnack pointed out, if Christ came merely to demonstrate the love of God, there is no real necessity for the cross, and none even for the incarnation. In addition, the theory fails to deal with the problem of guilt. Nevertheless, it has two merits that ought to be recognized. (1) The first relates to the emphatic position that Abelard gave to the love of God as the operative factor in the atonement. Everyone agrees that the institution of the atonement is to be ascribed to the love of God, but Abelard surpasses all his predecessors and contemporaries in the consistency with which he sought to interpret the atonement in terms of love.

[2] Aulén, *Christus Victor.* S. P. C. K., London, 1931.

(2) The second is closely connected with the first. In interpreting the atonement as a work of the love of God which evokes a responsive love in the hearts of men, Abelard transposed it wholly to the subjective realm, and although this was an exaggeration, it was of value as a protest against the objectivism of those who saw in the atonement only a transformation of the human situation and were relatively indifferent to its bearing on the human condition. Kierkegaard's dictum, "Truth is subjectivity," can, of course, be misunderstood; properly understood, it says something that needs to be said, and Abelard deserves credit for having said it in his own way eight centuries before Kierkegaard.

Whereas the Abelardian theory saw the atonement as a movement that is directed from God toward man, the Anselmic or transactional type of theory which virtually attained the status of orthodoxy in both Rome and the churches of the Reformation, views it as a movement in the opposite direction from man toward God: Christ acts upon God in behalf of men in such a way that the forgiveness of God is made available to them. In its Anselmic, quasi-feudal form Christ pays the debt men owe to God for their failure to accord him the honor due to him in virtue of his station; in its later, Calvinistic, more juridical form, Christ suffers the penalty, to which men are liable for their sin, and so satisfies the justice of God. The view is open to several objections.

1. It is inconsistent with the New Testament, which uniformly represents the atonement as a movement, of which God is not only the originator but the active agent, and which he directs toward man: "God so loved the world, that he gave his only begotten Son. . . . God was in Christ, reconciling the world unto himself. . . . Whom God put forward as an expiation by his blood. . . . He [God] made him to be sin who knew no sin" (John 3:16; II Cor. 5:19; Rom. 3:25; II Cor. 5:21). When the initiative is ascribed more particularly to Christ and his action is conceived as directed upon God, it be-

comes difficult to avoid the implication, all too plain in Anselm, that "God the Father and God the Son represent . . . different moral qualities, justice and love or mercy."[3] In the New Testament the Father and the Son are of one heart and mind.

2. The most serious objection concerns the idea of satisfaction that is central to every form of the theory: forgiveness is held to be contingent upon satisfaction made in some form or another to the justice of God by Christ on man's behalf. But is it then really forgiveness at all? The presupposition of all theories of this type is that the order of law and justice is inviolable, and that free forgiveness would be prejudicial to it. What Christ is thought to have accomplished by his atoning work is not a relaxation of the law in favor of men but only a diversion of its incidence. Nothing could be farther from the truth than the allegation sometimes made that the theory represents Christ as inducing a change in God's attitude toward sinners. God's attitude does not change; his law remains "the backbone, the skeleton, the granite foundation of the spiritual world," as Brunner expresses it.[4] But the requirements of God's law are so fully met by Christ that divine justice is *satisfied* and sinners are thereby exempted from its operation. Every variation of the theory is an attempt to find a *satisfactory* conception of the work of Christ, i.e., one that may plausibly be deemed capable of satisfying the requirements of the justice of God: the discharge of men's debt, the suffering of the penalty, the rendering of perfect obedience, the consummation of penitence, the perfect Amen in humanity to the judgment of God upon human sin — each of these formulas is an attempt to find the value of x which will make it equal to y in the equation between the work of Christ and the requirement of God.[5] But if the factors in the atonement

[3] J. K. Mozley, *op. cit.*, p. 130.

[4] *Der Mittler*, p. 414. Mohr, Tübingen, 1927.

[5] This suggestion was derived from Moberly's criticism of Anselm's theory, that it could be readily translated into arithmetical terms. Substitute algebraical for arithmetical terms and the criticism becomes wide enough to include many others, its author among them.

can be reduced to an equation, there is no place for forgiveness at all; the whole thing has become "a matter of commutative justice, of *quid pro quo*."[6] The Anselmic theory, which appears to be more successful than any other in explaining the possibility of forgiveness, really explains it away. According to the New Testament, forgiveness is the free gift of God and its only ground is his grace who bestows it.

3. The use of the idea of satisfaction in this theory further intensifies the difficulty of substitution. The difficulty is not so great perhaps when the atoning act is construed as the payment of a debt, as it was by Anselm, but it becomes intolerable when the conception is that of suffering punishment. Justice is sometimes portrayed as a blindfolded figure; but the justice that is "satisfied" if only punishment be inflicted, regardless of whether it be on the innocent or the guilty, is blind indeed. And the difficulty is not relieved by appeal to the willingness of Christ to suffer in our room and stead, since the crux of the matter is the transaction between the Father and the Son, and it is impossible to escape the thought of the Father inflicting punishment in the interests of justice upon his own guiltless Son. Calvin saw clearly that this thought was demanded by the logic of the theory; yet even he shrank back from it, and tried to temper it with a transparent sophistry: "We do not admit God was ever hostile to him, or angry with him. For how could he be angry with his beloved Son in whom his soul delighted, or how could Christ by his intercession appease the Father for others, if the Father were incensed against him? But we affirm that he sustained the weight of the divine severity, since, being smitten and afflicted of God, he experienced from God all the tokens (*omnia signa*) of wrath and vengeance."[7] If the justice of God could be satisfied with a token-punishment, the whole argument is unhinged.

4. This type of theory, while construing the atonement as

[6] Charles Hodge, *Systematic Theology,* II, p. 470. Charles Scribner's Sons, 1872–1873.

[7] *Inst.,* II, 16. 11.

an act directed from man toward God, is usually emphatic in ascribing its initiation to God. It is the mercy and love of God that institutes the whole arrangement for the salvation of sinners. But the arrangement itself is worked out as a matter of justice, and in this way, according to the theory, both the integrity of the divine mercy and that of the divine justice are preserved. There are two flaws in this ingenious scheme. If forgiveness for men can be procured only by means of an arrangement that conforms to the order of justice, the act of mercy that institutes the arrangement is itself out of order; the justice of God must surely exclude such an act of mercy just as it excludes an act of unconditional forgiveness. Again, it is doubtful if the arrangement itself can be held to be in strict accordance with justice in view of the substitution of Christ for sinners. Anselm was at pains to demonstrate the justice of Christ's free disposal of the benefits of his atoning death among his needy brethren: "I think," says Boso, with Anselm's concurrence, "it would be both just and necessary that the gift of salvation should be given by the Father to whomsoever the Son wished; because the Son should be allowed to give away what is his own." [8] But there is a manifest equivocation in the argument; the justice that gives a man freedom to dispose of his own as he may choose is of a different kind from the justice that Anselm invokes at an earlier stage to support the argument that the unconditional remission of sins by God would be an irregularity.[9] The Son enjoys a range of freedom that is denied to the Father; yet since the Father both instigates and approves the action of the Son, he countenances an irregularity, though himself incapable of it. It is only the appearance of justice that is preserved by means of a legal artifice.

The persistent popularity of this type of theory, however, is an indication that there is something in it that makes a powerful appeal to the human heart. Anselm himself laid his finger

[8] *Cur Deus Homo,* II, 19. [9] *Op. cit.,* I, 12.

on this something when he met the suggestion of Boso, that a feeling of repentance should be sufficient to blot out at least a minor sin, with the famous rejoinder, "You have not taken into account how grave a thing sin is" (*Nondum considerasti quanti ponderis sit peccatum*).[10] The theory rests upon a profound estimate of the gravity of sin and a conviction that it is not easily to be disposed of. It is radically opposed to the lighthearted attitude that would regard forgiveness as a matter of course and make grace "cheap," as Bonhoeffer has put it. The varied efforts that have been made to establish an equivalence between the work of Christ and the forgiveness of God represent a determination to exhibit the "costliness" of grace. All presuppose that forgiveness is a problem that has to be worked out and that it can be worked out only by God. With this there will be fairly general agreement. The questionable aspect of the theory is the assumption, introduced by Anselm, and tacitly accepted by his successors, that the root of the problem is in God and that it consists in his having to find an equation between his mercy and his justice, in virtue of which he can extend mercy without prejudice to his justice. This conception that forgiveness presents a kind of dilemma to God, who has to devise a way in which he can exercise mercy under guise of justice, without letting his left hand know what his right hand doeth, is, as we have already noted, completely at variance with the New Testament which nowhere suggests that forgiveness is a problem for God.

One of the principal differences between the ancient or "classic" theory of the atonement, to which we now turn, and the Anselmic theory is in its view of the problem, which it locates, not in God who extends forgiveness, but in the situation of man to whom forgiveness is extended. This underlies the further difference regarding the direction of the atoning work of Christ, which is thought of, not as a transaction with the Father, but as a victorious conflict with the powers that

[10] *Cur Deus Homo,* I, 21.

determine the human situation. God attacks the problem by sending his Son to effect a drastic change in the human situation; Christ, by his life and particularly by his death, won a decisive victory over Satan and the powers of evil, and so delivered men from their sway.

The theory, which has some support in the language of the New Testament, enjoyed great popularity in the ancient church, but in the West the difficulty of accepting it literally apparently began to be felt quite early. Its dramatic dualism and the absurdly imaginative accounts that some of the fathers gave of Christ's conflict with the powers of evil, which is obviously the point on which the theory turns, combined to bring it into disrepute, and Anselm's ruthless criticism virtually banished it from serious theological consideration, although there were some, like Luther, who continued to use its dramatic imagery. Fresh attention has, however, been directed to it in the present century by the Swedish theologians, Aulén and Nygren, who have attempted to rehabilitate it by distinguishing its fundamental motifs from the mythological trappings in which they are decked out. Viewed in this light, the theory exhibits a number of features that are deserving of notice. (1) It is evangelical to a unique degree; it sounds a note of triumph, which is in harmony with the Easter faith of the primitive church, more clearly and unequivocally than any other. (2) The conception of a battle between Christ and the powers of evil, although difficult to accept literally, reflects a sense of the seriousness and power of evil greater even than the Anselmic theory; its sees men in servitude to powers with which they are impotent to deal. And it is this situation which constitutes the problem.

Nevertheless there are difficulties in the theory that are not exclusively rooted in its original mythological character and that cannot be removed by any process of demythologization. (1) The conception of a victorious encounter between Christ and transcendent powers of evil has often been regarded with suspicion because of the implied dualism. It may be that a limited or provisional dualism is inescapable in Christian thought, as Aulén contends,[11] but even if this be conceded, there is still the difficulty that Satan and the powers of evil have not noticeably relaxed their sway over the lives of men. The triumph of Christ over all evil is the object of Christian hope, which looks to it as the ultimate consequence of his historic work; it can hardly be regarded as the real content of his historic work. (2) The theory conceives the work of Christ in an extremely objective manner as a transformation of the human situation, but it gives it no direct bearing on the (subjective) human condition. The battle takes place over man's head; he is, at most, a spectator of it but, he is not involved in it; and he is presented with the victory as a *fait accompli.* Now, it is true that in the atonement Christ does something for us that we cannot do for ourselves, but it is a question whether he does it quite so apart from us and without us, as the theory represents. This points to the third difficulty. (3) The theory does not attach any essential significance to the humanity of Christ. Since the powers of evil are of more than human stature, it is only a more than human power that can overcome them. Christ is indeed the champion of men, but essentially the divine champion. There seems to be no necessity for the incarnation.[12]

There is a certain affinity between the classic theory and the theory recently advanced by Karl Barth. Barth's interpretation of the work of Christ, which is developed with great power and impressiveness,[13] employs for the most part the

[11] Aulén, *The Faith of the Christian Church,* pp. 201 ff.

[12] Aulén maintains that the manhood of Christ receives full emphasis in the classic theory, but at the same time he admits that "the conflict and triumph of Christ is God's own conflict and triumph; it is God who in Christ reconciles the world to himself" (*Christus Victor,* p. 168). In the ancient church the manhood of Christ was necessary only for the deception of the devil. The decisive factor was always the divinity.

[13] *KD,* IV, 1.

juridical concepts of the "penal-substitutionary" theory, but it combines them in an original manner with others that point more in the direction of the classic theory. The reason for this is that Barth is engaged throughout in a polemic against Bultmann's program of demythologization, and he has therefore a special concern to stress the objective nature of the atonement as a real transformation of the human situation, in opposition to Bultmann, who would reduce it to a subjective alteration in man's understanding of his existence.[14] Of course, Barth does not attempt to rehabilitate the mythological concept of a victorious battle between Christ and Satan, but in effect he transposes it to an ontological key and opposes it as such to the purely existential interpretation of Bultmann. At the same time he is perfectly willing to acknowledge the subjective aspect of the atonement, with which Bultmann is concerned, viz., its bearing on the experience of those who accept the Christian message; he insists, however, that the Christian message, the kerygma, is primarily a message about Jesus Christ and about something that was done decisively, once and for all, by him, and only secondarily and consequently a message concerning ourselves. He does not mean that the atonement is the creation of a possibility or the offer of an opportunity, which is then literally followed by our subjective appropriation of it; he makes the subjective and the objective inseparable, and almost coincident, by making the atonement an ontological event in which our existence is really involved from the outset. The transition from the objective to the subjective does not represent a sequence in the reality of the atonement; it is merely a sequence in our understanding of two aspects of the reality, which are inseparable.[15]

The union of objective and subjective in this way is made possible by Barth's combination of juristic with ontological concepts. Briefly stated, the core of his interpretation is as fol-

[14] *KD*, IV, 1, Vorwort; cf. pp. 95 f.; p. 273.
[15] *KD*, IV, 1, pp. 311 ff.

lows: The Son of God, when he became man, entered into the human situation and took our place as sinners; he took it, not to do what we do in it, but to take the responsibility for what we do. He effected a real exchange; when he took the responsibility for our sin, he took it away from us, and it is no longer ours. We are really separated from our sin; we are "displaced persons"; our being as sinners has no future. Christ, then, having taken the place of us sinners, accomplishes the judgment of sin by submitting to it himself. He goes our way, the way of sinners, right to its bitter end in death, destruction, and the boundless misery of exclusion from God, and in so doing he delivers sinful man together with his sin, in his own person, to the nothingness or nonbeing, to which it belongs. "One can also say," adds Barth, "that he accomplishes this judgment by enduring the punishment which we have all incurred."[16] But Barth finds the idea of punishment inadequate to express the decisive thing, which is that Christ, by going to death for us has in his own person made an end of us as sinners and of sin itself; he has canceled, negated, annihilated us, along with our sin and the condemnation that belongs to it. The Passion of Christ was necessary, because sin could only be eliminated by allowing it to work itself out to its final consequence in eternal death – not because of the inexorable vengeance of God, but because of the radical nature of his love, which could only be "satisfied" by the complete execution of his wrath against the man of sin, by his extinction, elimination, and death. Barth will only admit the problematical conception of satisfaction (i.e., doing enough) in the sense that God himself in the Passion of his Son has done enough to eliminate sin and restore order between himself, the Creator, and his creation. The Passion of Christ is not only our judgment, but our annihilation; since he went to the cross in our place, we are crucified with him; we are done away with; our existence has now no object and no future. Christ has taken our being as sinners

[16] *KD*, IV, 1, p. 278.

and cast it behind him. His death was the death of us all, and this is true prior to our acceptance or response or "existential" involvement or even to our hearing of it in the kerygma.

That the death of Christ does not prove the final end of us – that is the meaning of the resurrection and the new being in Christ. But it is not necessary, for our present purpose, to pursue this side of the matter. Enough has been said to indicate the main features of Barth's interpretation and to enable us to ask whether he has been successful in overcoming the difficulties that we have already noted in the two lines of thought that he combines.

Barth's interpretation has the merit, which it shares with the classic theory to which it is related, that it sees the root of the problem in the situation of sinful men. The necessity of the atonement arises, not from the inexorable requirements of the justice of God which must be satisfied before he can exercise mercy, but from the objective realities of the situation which has been created by sin. In an interesting and important passage Barth analyzes the situation and discusses the relation between sin, reconciliation, and death.[17] Human sin is the disturbing factor in creation; it is the obstacle, which disrupts the covenant relation between God and man, and reconciliation, therefore, involves the removal of sin. At the same time sin is the source of the destruction and death that threaten man, and reconciliation, therefore, involves also the stopping up of this source. Reconciliation, that is to say, must eliminate sin in its double character as rebellion against God and as the ground of man's doom.

The dual aspect of the situation underlies Barth's dual interpretation of the work of Christ and his use of both juridical and ontological categories. The former he applies to the work of Christ in its relation to the responsibility and guilt of sin, the latter in its relation to the ensuing doom; but he relates them in a manner that is puzzling and unconvincing. On

[17] *KD,* IV, 1, p. 278.

the one hand he allows that we are relieved of our responsibility for sin when Christ, incarnate as "the man for other men," stepped into our place and took it upon himself; but on the other hand he repeatedly affirms that the decisive thing is that in his death Christ effected the ontological annihilation of us sinners together with our sin. He seeks in this way to stress the objective nature of the work of Christ while at the same time conserving the subjective aspect of our involvement in it. But it is a question whether the transition that Barth appears to make from the juridical to the ontological is legitimate. How can the juridical act of Christ in submitting to the judgment of sin produce the ontological effect of annihilating sin? And if the ontological is decisive, if, in other words, annihilation is the only way in which sin can be removed, we are driven back on the thought of some necessity in God – whether it be justice or love – which, like an Atlantic hurricane, must blow itself out.[18] Moreover, if the exchange or substitution of Christ means our displacement as persons, the subjective is swallowed up in the objective. It is not our guilt that is removed from us, but we are removed together with our guilt; in the vulgar saying, the baby is emptied out with the bath water.

The final, and, for our present purpose, the most important question to be raised regarding Barth's interpretation of the atoning work of Christ is what significance it ascribes to the incarnation. It was a weakness of the classic theory, as we observed, that the humanity of Christ plays only a minor and instrumental role in it; the decisive factor is the divinity. Barth lays great emphasis on the humanity; he dwells on it at length and illuminates it in several ways. He contends that the incarnation with its attendant humiliation must not be thought of as an act that involves a *kenosis* of divinity or renunciation of the attributes of Godhead, but rather as an authentic expression of Godhead, an act of obedience to the essential nature of God. He finds in the Gospel records of the historical life of

[18] *KD*, IV, 1, p. 280.

Jesus as the man for other men an important clue to the substitution or exchange that is involved in his atoning work. Yet here too the humanity is only instrumental; it was from his divinity that Christ derived the authority and the power to effect the exchange.[19] And although he became man in order to suffer as man the judgment due to man for his sin, his human Passion derives its uniqueness only from his divinity; it is the divine person of the sufferer that gives this Passion " a real dimension of depth " which reaches to the ontological root of sin, and a significance that is not only for the immediate historical situation, in which it occurred, but for the whole world of mankind.[20] But if it is only the divine Christ who is able both to detach our sin from us and reduce it to nothingness, is there any real necessity for him to become man and go through the painful and humiliating juridical procedure at the human level? Is a divine redeemer not sufficient to work the salvation of men, if the salvation of men depends on an ontological encounter with nothingness, any less than if it depends on a mythological encounter with Satan and the powers of darkness?

Barth's interpretation of the work of Christ has been discussed at this length because it illustrates very clearly that the place that is given to the humanity of Christ in the atonement is determined by the analysis of the problem. If the problem is analyzed in ontological terms, if sin is defined as an " ontological impossibility " or " un-thing," the solution must also take an ontological form, i.e., the removal of sin must consist in its annihilation. And if the annihilation of sin is held to involve the annihilation of the sinner, such language, which follows a prominent strain in the New Testament, is defensible and readily intelligible; for sin, however objectively conceived, is always attached to a personal subject, and the annihilation of sin may therefore be said to involve the " displacement " of the subject (" the old man ") and his replacement by a new

[19] *KD,* IV, 1, p. 244.

[20] *KD,* IV, 1, pp. 271 f.

subject ("the new man"). It is doubtful, however, whether this mode of language bears in the New Testament the decisive significance that Barth finds in it. Paul informs his readers on more than one occasion that they are dead, and then, paradoxically, proceeds to exhort them to live accordingly (Rom., ch. 6; Col., ch. 3). Indeed, he goes farther; he calls upon his readers themselves to put off the old man and put on the new (Eph. 4:22 ff.). The truth is that the decisive fact of Christian experience can be expressed in a variety of ways or at a variety of levels; it can be expressed in terms of a break in the continuity of the self; it can be expressed in terms of an underlying continuity of the self; [21] and different modes of expression can be combined in a paradoxical way. The classic example of this is Paul's statement in Gal. 2:20: "I am crucified with Christ: nevertheless I live; yet not I, but Christ liveth in me: and the life which I now live in the flesh I live by the faith of the Son of God, who loved me, and gave himself for me." Paul here oscillates among three modes of expression, one in terms of personal displacement, one in terms of personal union, and the third in terms of personal relationship (for faith is evidently understood as a relationship in which the personal subject or self plays a vital role). And there are others that could be used, as he does elsewhere, to express the central fact of Christian experience at other levels; e.g., to name the most obvious, there is the psychological, which expresses the Christian experience in terms of an alteration of consciousness. All of these, and others, are used in the New Testament, and we have no right to select one, to assign it a decisive significance, and to declare that it alone corresponds to the authentic interpretation of the work of Christ. The history of the doctrine of the atonement is a long record of attempts to find one single key that will unlock the mystery. But the effect, as we have tried to demonstrate, has been to concentrate undue significance on one aspect of the total fact of Christ, as it is pre-

[21] Barth can also do it this way; cf. *KD*, IV, 1, pp. 665 f.

sented in the New Testament, and to abbreviate or obscure the rest. And it is the humanity or human life of Christ that has been lost to sight for the most part. During the heyday of the classic and juridical theories, it was either passed over completely as having no bearing on "the substance of our redemption," as Calvin put it; or it received a minor and instrumental role: if Christ could do what he did only because he was God, why did he have to become man in order to do it? When Schleiermacher put forward a psychological account of the Christian salvation as an alteration of consciousness and interpreted the work of Christ accordingly, he gave a decisive significance to the human life of Christ – but again it was at the cost of reducing other aspects to relative insignificance: as is well known, Schleiermacher had no use for the resurrection and ascension of Christ. This does not mean that Schleiermacher's psychological approach was wrong; on the contrary, the dogma of the humanity of Christ surely demands it; for the psychological is an essential element in the truly human, and if the humanity of Christ is taken seriously, the Christian salvation must have its psychological aspect. Only, the fact that Schleiermacher virtually eliminated other aspects of the fact of Christ, which play an important part in the New Testament, is an indication that the significance of the humanity of Christ itself is too narrowly conceived when salvation is reduced to psychological terms.

Schleiermacher's interpretation of the atonement belongs to the type that is classified as subjective. He sees salvation as a change in consciousness, and this is for him the guarantee of its authenticity; for the basic principle of all his thinking is that that is real which is real to consciousness. The type of theory which is classified as objective, and of which we may take Barth's as an example, seeks to guard against the obvious weaknesses of the subjective position by stressing the objectivity of the atonement: so Barth, as we have seen, interprets it as a transformation of the human situation that is objectively real prior to our consciousness of it, though he seeks to do justice to the subjective aspect by including our existence in the situation that is transformed. But the reality of the transformation is of an ontological order, and, as such, beyond the reach of empirical observation.

This antithesis, in which we discern the fateful legacy of Kantianism, can be overcome only when we recognize that the basic reality of human existence is being in relation to others, a reality in which the subject-object antithesis is transcended from the outset. The division of this reality into two opposite poles is an artificial putting asunder of what God has joined together. It is surprising that both Schleiermacher and Barth should allow their thinking on the atonement to be influenced so largely by the antithesis of subjective and objective, since both are aware of the reality in which it is transcended. The alteration in consciousness, in which Schleiermacher saw the Christian salvation to consist, takes place when we are brought into relation to Christ, who " assumes believers into the power of his God-consciousness " and who institutes a " new corporate life." The transformation of the human situation, which Barth stresses, takes place likewise when Christ enters it and assumes the responsibility for our sin. It is strange that neither of them thought to find the decisive thing in the relation between Christ and sinful men itself rather than in its subjective effect in consciousness or its objective effect in the situation. It is especially strange in the case of Barth because when he seeks for the basic reality of human existence in the light of the archetypal humanity of Jesus, " the man for God," and " the man for other men," he finds it in its relatedness; indeed, he sees in the relatedness of human existence the image of God in man. Surely it is here in the relation between God and man that the decisive aspect of the atonement must be seen, and surely it is in terms of personal relationship that its ultimate mystery must be expressed. Neither Schleiermacher nor Barth, it may be observed, has much to say of forgiveness or reconciliation. For Schleiermacher reconciliation is defined as Christ's assumption of believers into the fellowship of his unclouded blessedness – an oddity of terminology that has often been remarked.[22] Barth makes only infrequent reference to forgiveness, which he defines as "the judicial act in which God has confirmed and asserted his own honor over against man."[23] Nowhere does he treat it as a transformation of the relation between God and man itself. The forgiveness or remission of sin is interpreted in a literal sense as the elimination of sin, the removal of an obstacle to the right relation between God and man, not as the establishment of the relation. The relation between God and man is, indeed, changed, and changed in a decisive way, but this change is the indirect result of an act of God that makes its direct impact elsewhere at a point in the background.

Barth's interpretation reflects a profound sense of the reality and gravity of sin as a factor that has a determinative influence on the relation between God and man; but when he sees the decisive aspect of God's act in Christ in the elimination of sin and makes the rectification of the relation between God and man contingent upon that, he reverses the emphasis of the New Testament, which gives the primacy to the positive impact of the act of God on the relation between him and man, and makes the negation of sin incidental to it. "God was in Christ, reconciling the world unto himself, not imputing their trespasses unto them": the reconciliation is the fundamental and decisive thing, and the nonimputation of sin is incidental to it; it is the reconciliation which alone makes the nonimputation possible and credible. This is the import of the New Testament message of the *grace* of God. Unless the primacy is given to reconciliation, the ultimacy of grace is impugned; grace is conceived as operating in the guise of a judicial act, and the consequence is that we are not directly touched by

[22] *The Christian Faith,* § 101.

[23] *KD,* IV, 1, p. 100.

grace — we are only the beneficiaries of a complex juridical process that is initiated by grace. But this is to deny the sufficiency of grace.

The plain sense of the gospel of grace, as it is presented in the New Testament, is that the object of the incarnation is to bring men into a personal relationship with God. It is to this end that the apostle declares the word of life, which he has heard and seen and looked upon and handled: "That ye also may have fellowship with us: and truly our fellowship is with the Father, and with his Son Jesus Christ" (I John 1:3). This is the heart of the Christian salvation, and the incarnation was essential to its accomplishment. There are other things that God can do, and does, for men without incarnation. If for this thing he became incarnate — "Who for us men and for our salvation came down from heaven, and was incarnate by the Holy Ghost of the Virgin Mary, and was made man" — clearly our salvation is of such a nature that it could only be accomplished in our humanity; it had to be lived humanly into our life. This is the nature of personal relations. We can have no truly personal relation except with one who meets us at our own level, one who is *homo-ousios* with us, one whose approach to us is made in freedom and is reciprocated in freedom. We cannot have such a relation with an animal or an inanimate object that is unable to reciprocate, or that is entirely at our disposal. We also cannot have such a relation with God as God, for we are entirely at his disposal. But this is the measure of the grace of God, that he who in the power of his Godhead can dispose of us as he will, who can transform our situation, who can alter our consciousness, condescends to assume our humanity, to meet with us humanly and deal with us in human terms, in order to establish with us a truly personal relationship and so to determine our existence in the most fundamental way.

It is here, in the encounter of the incarnate Christ with men that the decisive event took place — not in some metaphysical transformation of the situation beneath the level of existence, but in the establishment of a new relationship at the level of existence. It was the mission of Christ to be the human agent of this purpose of God, and his whole life is the record of his fulfillment of it. By his life among men and for men he wrought salvation for them; salvation was not a result of something he did in entering humanity or of something he did in dying a human death; it was the work of his life and his death to relate himself freely to men and them to himself: and this relation is the core and foundation of their salvation.

This relation is also the authentic expression and work of the grace of God. The grace of God is his will to have fellowship with sinful men, and its primary work is to be seen, not in the removal of the obstacle to that fellowship, but in the establishment of the fellowship that removes the obstacle. Christ is the human agent of this divine grace; he is the man who came to bring to men the forgiveness of God. To think of Christ as one who came to work out some problem and so make forgiveness possible is to deny the sufficiency of grace: he came as the bearer of forgiveness, which is the gift of the grace of God from all eternity. He dispensed forgiveness to men from the beginning of his public ministry, with never a suggestion that it was contingent upon any work he did, but only that it was present in him in a unique way. Nor did he ever suggest that only with his mission had God begun to be gracious, or that there had been no forgiveness for men before he came. Any such suggestion would be utterly at variance with the message of the Old Testament. The men of the Old Testament knew from the beginning of God's dealings with them that he is a forgiving God. Indeed the closest approximation to a creedal statement in the Old Testament is the passage, seven times repeated in almost identical terms, that proclaims the God of Israel as "the Lord, the Lord God, merciful and gracious, long-suffering, and abundant in goodness and truth" (Ex. 34:6; Neh. 9:17; Ps. 86:15; 103:8; 145:8; Joel 2:13; Jonah

4:2). The men of Israel never doubted that there is forgiveness with God; they never asked how it is possible for God to forgive; they never imagined that forgiveness posed some kind of problem for God. The problem was on their side, the problem of where to find God; for forgiveness is the free gift of God and can be received only at his hand and realized in a personal relationship with him. So, when Christ extended the forgiveness of his sins to the paralytic, it was not the possibility of forgiveness that was disputed by the scribes but Christ's assumption of the right to dispense it (Mark 2:1–12). This was the novelty of the mission of Christ that in him the forgiveness of God was present in person and extended to men in a human personal relationship. And even this was not utterly novel; for the mediatorial role of "the man of God" in the old covenant foreshadowed, and was fulfilled in, the coming of the man in whom God was present personally, "the one mediator between God and men, the man Christ Jesus" (I Tim. 2:5).[24] Forgiveness belongs by its nature to the realm of personal relationships; it cannot be effected by cultic or legal or ethical procedures (although they may point to it – Heb. 9:9); it is essentially an act in which a person relates himself to another freely, transcending all norms. It can never be traced to any premises and grounded in any "Because." Its keyword is always "Nevertheless"; its only ground is the unfathomable grace of God and its extension to men in personal relationship in the life of the man in whom God is personally present.

There are three questions that may be asked concerning this view from the standpoint of the traditional approach to the doctrine of the atonement.

1. The first has to do with the relation of forgiveness to the justice or righteousness of God. This is, of course, the central problem of the satisfaction theory of Anselm and all its various derivatives, including that of Barth. The idea of satisfaction implies that there is no possibility of forgiveness except where

[24] Cf. Barth, *KD,* I, 2, pp. 90 ff.

the requirements of justice are satisfied; and all the varied conceptions of satisfaction, feudal, penal, ethical, cultic, etc., are so many attempts to propound a way in which the righteous judgment of God upon sin is executed and at the same time a way is opened for forgiveness. If the forgiveness of God is extended to men in Jesus Christ in the manner we have suggested, how are the requirements of his justice satisfied? How can God forgive and at the same time maintain the order of his Kingdom, as Anselm puts it? The question presupposes that forgiveness and justice are opposite and incompatible, and that they cannot both be exercised at the same time. Occasionally, indeed, the extreme view has been taken that the one excludes the other absolutely. At the time of the Reformation there were some who, in the first flush of enthusiasm for the rediscovered gospel of forgiveness by free grace, felt bound to maintain that there could be no place for the law of righteousness in Christian faith. The problem of the relation between the law and the gospel became a crucial one for the Reformers, who expended much ingenuity on it.[25] But though they found no less than three distinct " uses of the law," they were not able to overcome the presupposition of a radical contradiction between them. Their solution of the problem proposed an alternation between law and gospel, rather than a reconciliation; they allowed law to operate outside, and before, and after, the gospel, but not with it.

The problem is presented in its most acute form by the evangelical records of the ministry of Jesus. Jesus both proclaimed and dispensed the gospel of forgiveness and at the same time demanded unconditional obedience to the law of righteousness. Various attempts have been made to resolve the apparent contradiction. It has been suggested that the obedience which Jesus demands is vicariously rendered by him-

[25] Luther, who wrestled long and earnestly with this problem, once said, " Whoso can rightly judge between the law and the gospel, let him thank God and know that he is a right divine " (*WA*, 40, 1, p. 206; *Commentary on Galatians*, ET, 1953, p. 122).

self.[26] But this view appears forced, in face of the actual terms of Jesus' demands, which have all the air of categorical imperatives: Resist not evil . . . love your enemies . . . be ye perfect . . . seek first the kingdom of God and his righteousness – these are unmistakably commands which are meant to be obeyed by those to whom they are addressed. Jesus absolutizes the demands of the law in such a way as to strike dismay into the heart of even its most conscientious observer (Mark 10:22). There is a side to his teaching that repels (John 6:60–66) and terrifies (Luke 12:5). And this is not merely provisional or preliminary, as if the harsh note of law were finally superseded by the sweet melody of gospel. The message of the Son of Man retains the note of judgment to the end. Even at his final appearing he shows a face from which men seek to hide (Rev. 6:16), and speaks in a voice more dreadful than that of Sinai, "I never knew you: depart from me, ye that work iniquity" (Matt. 7:23).

It has also been suggested that Christ's preaching of the law belongs to the old dispensation, since the old dispensation was not superseded until he died and rose again, and the gospel of forgiveness, which belongs to the new dispensation, could not be proclaimed before it was established. "During his earthly life," writes Brunner, "before Good Friday and Easter, a great deal could not possibly be said which became possible afterward. In so far as there is something temporary even about the teaching of Jesus, it can only disappear when the depth and richness of the message of the Kingdom is fully disclosed in the message of the crucified and risen Lord." [27] The view that the teaching of Jesus has a provisional character is a logical, if not an inevitable consequence of a transactional view of the atonement; for if the forgiveness of God was procured by the death of Jesus on the cross, he would have had no right

[26] Cf. Thurneysen, *Die Bergpredigt*. Kaiser, München, 1936.

[27] E. Brunner, *The Christian Doctrine of Creation and Redemption*, p. 280. The Westminster Press, 1952.

and no ground to preach anything other than the law beforehand. But it is beset with insurmountable difficulties. If the teaching of Jesus is an *Interimsethik* in the sense suggested, the question arises, What measure of authority still pertains to it, or By what principle may it be revised and corrected? A more serious and more obvious objection to the view is that the implication that the teaching of Jesus was limited to law and ethics is at variance with the facts. As we have repeatedly observed, the note of gospel is sounded in the teaching of Jesus from the beginning; and not only is the gift of forgiveness by free grace proclaimed, but the unique role of Jesus himself in dispensing it is clearly indicated.[28] It is true that certain doctrinal interpretations of the manner of his mediation, which were elaborated later, are absent from the teaching of Jesus, but there are others that are suggested in words of his own and that are sufficient to set the fact of his mediation beyond doubt.[29]

Law and gospel go hand in hand in the teaching of Jesus. He proclaims the demands of righteousness in the Sermon on the Mount with unprecedented rigor, and at the same time he declares free forgiveness to sinners. But it is not only in his words; law and gospel are wedded together in his life and action, from which, indeed, his words should never be separated. Jesus appears as a man who stands on the side of the law – he is commonly taken for a rabbi – and represents in his own life the righteousness it requires. Himself unchallengeable in his sinlessness, he never condoned sin in others, never made light of it, never called it by any other name than its own. But all the while he stands on the side of sinful men, he "receives" them, he consorts with them, he becomes "the friend of publicans and sinners." Here is the miracle of forgiveness in action.

[28] Cf. the episode of the paralytic in Mark, ch. 2, which shows in a programmatic way that from the beginning of his ministry the issues were no other than "the person and work of Christ."

[29] "Ransom" (Mark 10:45) and "Covenant-blood" (Mark 14:24). The ransom idea was made much of in the early church.

Righteousness and sin are incompatible as oil and water and tend naturally to separate – the official champions of the law of righteousness among the Jews were the Pharisees, whose name means " the separate ones " – but in Jesus righteousness did not separate itself from sin; rather it sought it out. There was no blurring of the distinction between them, no mollifying of the judgment of righteousness on sin. But with the judgment there was forgiveness; for the judgment *was* forgiveness, and the forgiveness *was* judgment. This was the source of the conflict between Jesus and the official representatives of Jewish religion; they could not conceive of a judgment of sin that was not exclusive in its effect. Jesus wrought the miracle of the judgment of sin that is inclusive, the judgment that is linked to its consequence, not by the *Because* of human consistency, but by the *Nevertheless* of divine grace. He wrought this miracle, not by some arbitrary exercise of divine omnipotence, but by coming to us as God incarnate and relating himself to us humanly, so that through relation to him, in whom both are united, we should be confronted with the full measure of the requirement of righteousness and at the same time receive the free gift of forgiveness.

It may be added, by way of explanation, that we have sought to distil the element of truth contained in the view, widely held in the ancient church, that the salvation of men was accomplished by the incarnation. The view was that the Son of God, by assuming our human nature, and wearing it, so to speak, on his own sinless person, transmuted its substance and, in effect, deified it. But if the reality of humanity is to be found, not in its metaphysical substance, but in the personal relations in which we actually exist, if " the primary word is I and Thou," we cannot be saved by any miracle of transubstantiation, but only as we are taken into a personal relation with God in our actual existence. Therefore, if the incarnation be interpreted in the " existentialist " terms of the Biblical testimony rather than in the " essentialist " categories of Greek philosophy, if, that is to say, it be understood, not merely as the assumption of our nature, but as the living of the incarnate life in personal relations with men at the human level, then we may say with truth that salvation is by incarnation.

2. The second question concerns the significance of the death of Christ. The atoning work of Christ has from the beginning been associated in a decisive way with his death. The first article in the apostolic tradition that Paul inherited was that "Christ died for our sins" (I Cor. 15:3). The cross has always been the symbol of forgiveness to Christian faith, and it is to what happened there that the church has looked in its endeavors to plumb the mystery of the gospel. If, as we have suggested, the mediation of the divine forgiveness is to be looked for in the incarnate life of Christ in personal relations with men at the human level, are we not removing the accent from the death to the life in a way that marks a radical departure from the tradition? The answer is, on the contrary, that the view which is advanced here, so far from robbing the death of Christ of its significance, rather opens up a perspective from which its true and full significance can be seen. It is only a protest against the tendency to attach an exclusive significance to the death of Christ, which has bedeviled Western thought on the atonement.

The New Testament certainly assigns a decisive significance to the death of Christ, but we misunderstand its language if we take it to mean that his death is the only thing that matters. It is this misunderstanding which underlies the persistent efforts of Western theology to seek the clue to the meaning of the death of Christ in all sorts of places except the likeliest one, namely, his life; for if we associate the atonement in a narrow and exclusive manner with the death of Christ, we block off the most obvious way to understanding and condemn ourselves to speculative theorizing. The truth that is being increasingly recognized is that the death of Christ may not be separated from his life. His life and his death are all of a piece, and neither of them can be properly understood apart from the other. What Christ accomplished in his death is nothing other than he had done throughout his life; in it he finished the work that had been given him to do. His death was the consummation of his life, the cross the completion of the incarnation.

Why did Christ die? The answer of the transactional type of theory has been that he died in order that forgiveness might be made possible. But if we view his death in the context of his life and seek the clue to its meaning there, the answer we must give is that he died because forgiveness was actual, because it was present in him, in the personal relations of his incarnate life with men at the human level. The death of Christ is indeed involved in the forgiveness of sins, and that of necessity: "the Son of man must suffer" (Mark 8:31). But the suffering was not imposed upon him by God in order to satisfy the inexorable requirements of the divine justice. Its necessity is grounded in the nature of the divine forgiveness and the human reaction to it.

The simplest answer to the question why Christ died is that men put him to death. They rejected him and killed him because they hated him. Such behavior might be considered strange toward one who came among them as the bearer of the gift of forgiveness, and indeed, the welcome accorded him in the early days of his public ministry shows that men were not indisposed to receive the gospel of forgiveness. But the gospel was conjoined with the law, and the forgiveness of God which Christ brought was also the judgment of God; and this was his undoing. Those who were ready to welcome the gospel were alienated by the law that went with it, and those who were willing to receive the law were antagonized by the accompanying gospel; and thus Jesus was rejected by both sections of the people, both by the righteous who needed no repentance and by the sinners whom he called to repentance. Had he made party with the populace against the authorities, as seemed likely at one stage, or had he made party with the authorities against the populace, as some of them evidently hoped he would, he might have escaped death. But by the very nature of his mission he antagonized them both, and in the end both concurred in the verdict, "Away with him, crucify him!"

At the same time, the cross was his own free choice. Christ chose to die and died willingly, because death was inherent in his mission as the bearer of the forgiveness of God to men. Forgiveness has its reality in a personal relationship in which alienation is countered by an acceptance that transcends it. Opposition is opposed by a love that overcomes it. The encounter of divine grace and human sin has the nature of a collision, and as such it necessarily involves suffering. The cross marks the climax of this suffering. The satisfaction type of theory has seen in the death of Christ a suffering of the divine reaction against sin, either as an endurance by him of the punishment due to sin, or as a realization in his spirit of the divine judgment upon sin. It may be granted that something of the latter entered into the ordeal of Christ in his death; as "the man for other men," he must surely have felt the gravity of their condition more deeply than they themselves. But to construe this suffering as vicarious penitence and to ascribe to it as such a power of satisfaction, as McLeod Campbell and Moberly did, is to see it in the wrong perspective. The suffering of Christ is not the suffering of sin as it encounters the judgment of God; it is the suffering of the judgment of God as it encounters sin; for the judgment of God encounters sin in the form of forgiving grace. Christ is indeed the bearer of the divine judgment upon sin, and as such he suffers. But it is not as the victim of the divine judgment that he suffers; it is as the victim of sin, to which he delivers the divine judgment in the form of forgiveness. In other words, the necessity of his suffering is a necessity of grace, not of satisfaction; for the grace of God in forgiveness is exercised by incarnation, i.e., by his condescension to enter into personal relations with men at their level and thus, in consequence, to place himself in their power. This is the mystery and the miracle of grace, which overcomes rejection by accepting it and achieves victory by submitting to defeat. The death of Christ is, therefore, the necessary completion of his mission; the personal relationship in which he brought men the forgiveness of God could only be consummated in this way. His final exclusion from mankind in death was his final inclusion of mankind in forgiveness.

The death of Christ is, then, of truly decisive significance, not because he wrought salvation for us by it alone, but because it was the end and fulfillment of his life. In his death he finished the work that it was the mission of his incarnate life to perform.

The question may be asked whether this view of the death of Christ does not set it on the same level as that of others who have suffered in the name of forgiving love, and so, in effect, deny its uniqueness. Are there not others who have died, as he died, because they refused to retaliate, and countered evil with good? The answer is that in this respect the cross of Christ is not unique. Indeed, its nonuniqueness is an implicate of the incarnation. Christ would have been less than truly human if he had come only to live the life of man and not also to die their death.[30] And the grace of God in choosing incarnation as the method of imparting his forgiveness to men through personal relations with them at the human level would have been meaningless, had not death for others been known as a real human possibility, even if only a rare one (cf. John 15:13; Rom. 5:7). But he is unique who died on the cross; for he came from God as the bearer of the divine forgiveness, and he is known as such, not by his death, but by his resurrection from the dead. It is the resurrection that discloses the divine mean-

[30] The simultaneous crucifixion of the two malefactors with him points up the fact that the death Christ died was the common death of men.

ing of the cross and establishes its uniqueness; for the resurrection means that he who through his life and death brought men the forgiveness of God is the risen and everliving Lord who continues to bring it to us through the same means. This will be the theme of the next chapter.

3. The third question that may be raised here concerns the Christology implied in this view of the atonement. If the reality of forgiveness is found in the personal relations that the incarnate Christ established with men at the human level, does this not point in the direction of a kind of Monophysitism? The question must be considered because it has been raised by Karl Barth regarding the Christology of Wilhelm Herrmann, whose interpretation of the work of Christ has some similarities with that which is offered in these pages.[31] Herrmann laid emphasis on the humanity of Christ as the essential condition for a real encounter by us with God in the realm of existence to which we belong: "It is only out of life in history that God can come to meet us. . . . Through the man Jesus we are first lifted into a true fellowship with God. . . . Through the power of the man Jesus over us we experience the operation of God himself upon us."[32] Barth pronounces this doctrine Monophysite, and he finds it significant that Herrmann made no mention of Eutyches in his review of the classical Christology in his *Dogmatik*. He contends that it is not in the *man* Jesus as such that we encounter God, since nothing that is reality in the human sphere can reveal God. The question that must be addressed to Barth is whether his interpretation of the classical Christology – through the spectacles of Leo's *Tome* – would not make it impossible for us to speak of Christ as God *in* man. In his recent study of Chalcedon, R. V. Sellers has pointed out the important fact that there are two principles in Christology, which are recog-

[31] K. Barth, "Die dogmatische Prinzipienlehre bei Wilhelm Herrmann," in *Die Theologie und die Kirche*, p. 275. Kaiser, München, 1928.
[32] W. Herrmann, *op. cit.*, pp. 60 ff.

nized in the Chalcedonian Definition, and which he calls the principle of Christological confession and the principle of Christological inquiry.[33] The former, which was represented by the Alexandrian school of thought, is related to the fundamental Christian apprehension of Christ as Savior. "Implicit in the primitive kerygma, and basic to the great Christological formulas in the New Testament, is the Christian confession that Jesus Christ is the Son of God, living a human life and sharing our experiences – that he is one and the same Person, who, existing eternally with the Father, has now become man for man's salvation."[34] From this soteriological perspective the emphasis is on the fact that God was in Christ. The principle of Christological inquiry, which was represented by the Antiochenes, comes into operation with the need to define the relation of Godhead and manhood in Christ in such a way as to maintain the integrity of the basic Christian confession; and here the tendency is to emphasize the distinction of the two natures. But the necessity to speak of God *and* man, which arises from this perspective, cannot alter the fact that the primary truth of faith is God *in* man, "God in, and through, and as, man," as Moberly put it.[35] In the man Jesus, God is present, and in the human course of his life among men God is dealing with us. This is what the incarnation means. Any Christological interpretation that refuses to allow it to mean this was failed in its task.

~

There is one final point that ought to be emphasized here, although it is almost self-evident, because of its importance for our understanding of the nature of the church, with which we shall be occupied in the concluding chapter. If the forgiveness of God is extended to us in the incarnate life of Christ

[33] R. V. Sellers, *The Council of Chalcedon*, pp. xiii ff.
[34] *Ibid.*
[35] Moberly, *Atonement and Personality*, p. 96.

among us, it cannot be separated from him. It is ours always and only "through Jesus Christ our Lord"; for its reality is in the actual living of his life in personal relation with us. Forgiveness is the miracle of grace; it is true only as it happens, and it happens in the fact of Jesus Christ, who *is* the miracle of forgiveness personally present among men.[36] Its possibility is grounded exclusively in its reality in him. William Temple, in a well-known passage of his Gifford Lectures, described the day on which Descartes conceived his *cogito ergo sum* as the most disastrous day in the history of philosophical thought.[37] A comparable occasion in the history of theological thought might well be seen in that day when Anselm conceived the idea of demonstrating the necessity of atonement, *remoto Christo*, "leaving Christ out of view, as if nothing had ever been known of him."[38] It is true that the disaster is mitigated by the fact that Anselm's alleged demonstration *a priori* is manifestly informed by the knowledge of Christ which he was pretending to forget. But Anselm must be held responsible for originating the idea that the ultimate ground of forgiveness is to be sought in some principle that lies behind the fact of Christ, and so launching Western theology on its endless quest for a *theory* of the atonement. There can be no theory of the atonement that is other than the fact of the atonement; for the atonement is the miracle of grace that is wrought by the presence of Christ as God incarnate in personal relation with men. The miracle

[36] Cf. Charles Williams, *The Forgiveness of Sins*, p. 50. Centenary Press, 1942: "He became then Forgiveness in flesh; he lived the life of Forgiveness. This undoubted fact serves as a reminder that forgiveness is an act, and not a set of words. It is a thing to be *done*. . . . The birth of Forgiveness was the birth of something of flesh and blood, of brain and bone. It appeared in the world at a certain time and place—in the world which we know as time and place. And it proceeded to live a life characterized (we are to believe) by acts and words which, in their relation to men throughout, were precisely Forgiveness."

[37] W. Temple, *Nature, Man and God*, p. 57. The Macmillan Company, 1934.

[38] Anselm, *Cur Deus Homo*, Preface.

cannot be referred to a principle; its only ground is its actual occurrence. Christ did not make forgiveness possible; he bestows it on us.[39] The true theory of the atonement consists, therefore, in the rehearsal of the events in which it is accomplished. As Barth has said: "It is the history of the man Jesus . . . in which he is, and in which he is the eternal salvation of all men. Absolutely everything for the eternal salvation of all men depends on the fact that this history can be *told*."[40] The gospel is not an abstract truth that can be distilled from the history. "The New Testament," to quote Barth again, "teaches no truth, except that which consists in the Johannine *ego eimi*."[41] The truth of the gospel is the history of the incarnate Christ in the performance of his saving work.

[39] Herrmann, *op. cit.*, p. 140.
[40] *KD*, III, 2, pp. 528 ff.
[41] *Ibid.*

CHAPTER

VIII

The Extension of the Incarnation

THE FORGIVENESS of sins is the free gift of God in Jesus Christ. Its only ground is the grace of God, and its reality is his incarnation. His presence among men as the Son of Man, the man whose existence is for other men, is the presence of forgiveness. Forgiveness cannot be referred to any principle behind the incarnation. It is the miracle of the grace of God in Jesus Christ, who calls men to seek the righteousness of the Kingdom of God and who at the same time extends to them the forgiveness of God. We have forgiveness only in personal relation with God incarnate.

Kierkegaard was right, therefore, when he said that in order to be Christians we have to become contemporaneous with Christ. We can have no personal relation with one who is separated from us in time or in space, and who is known to us only as a memory or a picture. His presence is essential. The first disciples were keenly aware of this. The "farewell discourses" of the Fourth Gospel reflect the fear and dismay that filled them at the prospect of his imminent departure; to those who had enjoyed the experience of his presence, the thought of his absence was unendurable. And the piety of later ages has often looked back with envy to the happiness of those who were with him in the days of his flesh. The sentiment is expressed in a familiar children's hymn:

"I think when I read that sweet story of old,
When Jesus was here among men,
How he called little children as lambs to his fold,
I should like to have been with them then.

"I wish that his hands had been placed on my head,
That his arms had been thrown around me,
And that I might have seen his kind look when he said,
'Let the little ones come unto me.'"

It is expressed also in somewhat more poignant tones in some lines by Palgrave (of *Golden Treasury* fame):

"But, O dear Lord, we cry,
That we thy face could see!
Thy blessèd face one moment's space
Then might we follow thee!

"Dim tracts of time divide
Those golden days from me;
Thy voice comes strange o'er years of change;
How can we follow thee?"

This nostalgic longing for "one of the days of the Son of Man" reflects a profound realization that nothing can compensate for the living presence of Christ. But how can that presence be real to us when it now lies "in the dark backward and abysm of time"?

The problem of faith and history has been a major preoccupation of modern theology since the time of the Enlightenment. The Enlightenment cut the Gordian knot by severing the connection between faith and history. The proper objects of faith, it held, are "necessary truths of reason," and between these and "contingent facts of history" there is an "ugly broad ditch" that cannot be crossed. Once the rational truths are grasped by the understanding, the historical facts, which depend upon the testimony of others, may serve as illustrations, but are ultimately expendable. To Kant it was only the *idea* of Christianity that mattered, and if that was established, it was a matter of indifference whether Christ ever lived or not. Hegel attempted to bring about a remarriage of the ideal and the historical, but only by fusing them in a way that stripped the historical of its contingent actuality.

The rationalism of the Enlightenment was, in part, the product of a concern for the immediacy of faith; for one important difference between "necessary truths of reason" and "contingent facts of history" is that the former, being timeless, are equally accessible to all at all times, whereas the latter belong to one time, and only those who are historically contemporaneous with them can enjoy an immediate relation to them. The concern for immediacy was made more evident in the romantic movement, which also emerged from the womb of the Enlightenment. Both rationalism and romanticism were in revolt against traditionalism, which was characteristic of both Catholic and Protestant orthodoxy. Traditionalism asserted the decisive and indispensable character of the historical events, on which faith is grounded, but when it made these events as such the object of faith, it equated faith with mental acceptance of a historical tradition. Luther's complaint against Catholic traditionalism was that it gave faith a purely historical relation to its object.[1] And the same may be said of the traditionalism of Protestant orthodoxy, which arose when Luther's basic insight had been lost. There is, indeed, a difference: the link that connects faith with its distant object is now the infallible Bible, not the infallible church; but the relation of faith to its object remains basically of a historical order.[2]

[1] It was their not wholly ingenuous assumption that Luther shared this conception of faith which enabled the members of the Council of Trent to present their ludicrous caricature of the doctrine of justification by faith.

[2] Traditionalism was further weakened by the rise of historical criticism, which exposed the uncertainty of all historical traditions; and the erection of infallibilities was a symptom of a growing awareness of this.

It was this identification of faith with acceptance of a historical tradition which provoked the revolt of piety against orthodoxy, to which reference was made in the first chapter. This revolt is a feature of both Catholicism and Protestantism in the nineteenth century. In Catholicism it manifested itself in a proliferation of piety, which has not only escaped the control of dogmatic orthodoxy, but, in some of its recent developments, has itself acquired the control over it. In Protestantism the revolt has followed a somewhat more restrained course.[3] The direction was pointed by Schleiermacher, who assigned to piety, not, indeed, a power to generate new dogmas, but a regulative control over the established dogmatic tradition. The general effect has been a contraction of the tradition, or rather a discrimination between those elements in the tradition which have "a demonstrable and definite connexion with the religious affections"[4] and those which do not. The quest for "the essence of Christianity," which has occupied much of modern theology, is a series of attempts to apply this pragmatic principle of immediate relevance to piety.

The real significance of Herrmann's *Communion with God,* to which we referred in the first chapter, is that it marks the crisis of this theological pragmatism. A man of profound personal piety, Herrmann had inherited from Schleiermacher the conviction that piety is regulative of faith; not the acceptance of doctrines from others, but the experience of communion with God as a reality in our own lives was for him "the peculiarity and the starting point of the Christian religion." But Herrmann had become aware (largely through the study

---

But the fundamental weakness of traditionalism was discerned by the Reformers before the rise of historical criticism.

[3] The cleavage between faith and piety is made complete in principle when it is accepted as a matter of course, as would appear to be the case when people say, in the name of piety, that orthodoxy is not enough. But this attitude is not likely to be found among persons of theological responsibility.

[4] Schleiermacher, *The Christian Faith,* § 29, 3 (ET, p. 125).

of Luther) of the danger that piety, if itself unregulated by faith, might drift away from its evangelical moorings and get caught in a current of mysticism that would carry it toward the shoals of Catholicism. He saw this danger acutely present in a situation where piety tended to attach itself to the risen and exalted Christ rather than to the Christ of history; for the Christ of history is " the real Christ "; it is " in the historical event of Christ's life in the real world " that God came to save us, and therefore it is to this Christ that evangelical piety must be attached.[5]

The main difficulty in the way of the realignment of evangelical faith and piety was that of establishing a personal relation with the Christ of history. Herrmann proposed that the key was to be found in what he called " the inner life of Jesus "; it is by his inner life that Jesus becomes " an element in the reality in which we stand," and we are led into his presence and brought into personal relation with him. But what is " the inner life " of Jesus? It has been widely felt that Herrmann never succeeded in making clear what he meant by this concept, or how it is possible for the inner life of Jesus to cross " the ugly broad ditch " of twenty centuries and become a present fact in our experience.

Herrmann was surely right in asserting the centrality of the incarnation. He saw clearly that if God's decisive deed for the salvation of men was done in Christ incarnate, this Christ must be the center of evangelical piety; he must become contemporaneous with us and " real " to us. But his attempt to locate the clue to contemporaneity in one selected aspect of the incarnate life, to the exclusion of other aspects, seems arbitrary and capricious. This was another example of that fragmentation of the gospel, which has been the bane of Christendom from the beginning. If it is true, as we have contended, that the fundamental concern of theology today must be the wholeness of the gospel, then it would seem that the solution

[5] *Op. cit.*, p. 287.

to this problem should be sought, not in isolating one aspect of the incarnate life, but rather in seeing the incarnate life within its total context.

~

The incarnation belongs to history; it took place at a date in the distant past. This is so basic that it is enshrined in the Creed, in the phrase, " under Pontius Pilate." The incarnate life of Christ is separated from us by a yawning gulf of centuries. How, then, can this Christ become contemporaneous with us?

The first thing to be observed is that extension is inherent in the incarnation as such. For the essence of the incarnation is to be found, not merely in God's becoming a man by the assumption of our flesh, or in his becoming *man* by the impersonation of universal humanity, but in his coming to be " the man for other men " and living a life in personal relation with men that was consummated by his giving of himself for them. The life that he came to live in the body was by its nature a life that sought an expanding embodiment in a community. One of the earliest acts of his public ministry was his gathering around him a group of twelve men, " that they should be with him," as Mark puts it in simple but pregnant words (Mark 3:14). They were the first of the men whom he was to be *for*, the foundation stones of the community, the *ecclesia,* which he was to build around himself as the Son of Man. It is noteworthy that in the narrative of Matthew the word about the building of the church is followed immediately by the intimation of the Passion (Matt. 16:21); for it is as Jesus goes forward to fulfill the destiny of the Son of Man, to be the man for other men, that he builds his church. His being for them is the foundation and bond of their solidarity.

This is no less true after the withdrawal of his bodily presence, only it becomes true in a different way, a two-dimensional way. In the historical dimension his being for men becomes his *having been* for them. It is an inescapable consequence of the historical nature of the incarnation that it recedes into the past. Incarnation involves "intemporation," as Brunner has said; for humanity means (among other things) temporality. And since

> "Time, like an ever-rolling stream,
> Bears all its sons away,"

the Jesus of history becomes a memory and a tradition. Schleiermacher expressed an important element of the truth when he spoke of the "picture" of Jesus which the Christian community preserves and cherishes,[6] for if Jesus was truly a figure of history, then, like all figures of history, he must retire from the scene and survive as a picture in the minds of those who were his contemporaries. The Gospels are in fact such pictures of Jesus, drawn by eyewitnesses for the benefit of others. For the same reason we must also recognize an important element of truth in the view that stresses the aspect of historical succession in the church's relation to Christ. It is a necessary consequence of the historical reality and once-for-allness of the incarnation that the church can be regarded as the institution founded by Christ to take over his mission at his departure and continue it throughout the succeeding ages of history. This view of the church as the successor of a Christ who is no longer present is basic to "catholic" ecclesiology.[7] It has received its clearest and most candid expression in a verse of an Anglican hymn:

> "His twelve apostles first he made
> His ministers of grace;
> And they their hands on others laid,
> To fill in turn their place.

[6] *The Christian Faith,* § 88 (ET, p. 364). Herrmann could also speak of the picture or portrait of Jesus; *op. cit.,* p. 72, etc.

[7] For documentation see the author's *The Holy Spirit in Christian Theology,* pp. 55 ff. The Westminster Press, 1956.

"So age by age, and year by year,
His grace was handed on;
And still the holy church is here,
Although her Lord is gone." [8]

It is also suggested by the description of the church as "the extension of the incarnation," which has become common in modern theology, especially among Anglicans. The phrase reflects a sound appreciation of the centrality and finality of the incarnation. If God's decisive deed for the salvation of the world was accomplished in the historical life of the incarnate Christ, that deed must somehow be extended in history, if it is to become what Herrmann called "an element in the reality in which we stand"; and clearly it is the community which was formed around the incarnate Christ, and which has continued in existence to this day, that must be regarded as, in some sense, the bearer of the extension. This accords with the view of Christ himself who "founded the church" for this purpose, that through it what he had accomplished in his life might be extended to those who were not his immediate contemporaries – "that repentance and remission of sins should be preached in his name among all nations" (Luke 24:47). He regarded the mission of the apostles as an extension of his own (John 20:21), and the means by which those of later ages were to be brought into relation to him (John 17:20; Acts 1:8).

But the phrase, "the extension of the incarnation," contains a certain ambiguity and can be understood in a number of different ways. It can be taken to mean that Christ, having completed the work of his incarnate life, has now, so to speak, resigned or retired in favor of the church, which has replaced him and taken over his function. This is, basically, the position of the Roman Church, which regards itself as "vicar" or trustee for a Christ who is absent, if not dead. In Roman

[8] John Mason Neale, *Hymns A. & M.*, 352.

ecclesiology the chief emphasis is always on the foundation of the church by Christ and its unbroken historical continuity with the apostolate; for it is by the legitimacy of its apostolic succession that the church is authenticated as the successor of (and substitute for) Christ. To most who speak of the church as the extension of the incarnation, however, the phrase conveys the thought of the continued presence of Christ rather than his absence, and sometimes this is expressed in terms of a certain identity between Christ and the church. The Anglo-Catholic group who wrote the study on Catholicity referred to the church as "a continuous historical society, whose essence is despite the imperfections of its members, the glorified humanity of our Lord."[9] Archbishop Gregg's paper on the church, which he presented to the Amsterdam Assembly of the World Council of Churches, began with the categorical statement, "The church is the extension in time and space of the incarnate Word of God, crucified, ascended, glorified, operating among men through the indwelling in them of his Holy Spirit, who mediates to it his victorious life."[10] And a recent papal encyclical quotes with approval the statement of Bellarmine that "the church is, as it were, another Christ."[11]

Such language, which has a long history in the Christian church, is intelligible as an attempt to express the closeness of the union between Christ and the church, of which Paul speaks. Just as in marriage husband and wife are said to become "one flesh," so Christ by his love for the church has made it one with himself. This "great mystery," as Paul called it (Eph. 5:32), has fascinated many of the greatest minds in Christendom, and some of them have been moved to express it in extravagant terms.[12] It was (surprisingly, it may appear

[9] *Catholicity*, p. 26. Dacre Press, 1947.

[10] John A. F. Gregg, "One, Holy, Catholic, Apostolic Church" in *Man's Disorder and God's Design*, I, p. 59. Harper & Brothers, 1948.

[11] *Mystici Corporis* (National Catholic Welfare Conference edition), p. 21. 1943.

[12] Cf. E. Mersch, *The Whole Christ* (Bruce Publishing Co., 1938), for the history of the idea.

to some) a favorite theme with Calvin, for whom it was a central element in the gospel, that the Christ, who is offered to us, has engrafted us into his body and united us to himself in what he calls a "sacred marriage" and a "mystical union."[13] But Calvin saw clearly that the vitality of the gospel and the evangelical power of the union between Christ and his church depend on the maintenance of the distinction between them; he was careful, therefore, to avoid any kind of language that would suggest a union of essence between them.[14]

Some, however, who speak of the extension of the incarnation, use it in a different sense. Bishop Gore, who appears to have been the first English theologian to describe the church in this phrase, wrote: "It was pointed out that there cannot be more than one incarnate Son of God: but it is also true that what was realized once for all in Jesus is perpetuated in the world. The church is the body of Christ. It is the extension and perpetuation of the incarnation in the world. It is this because it embodies the same principle and lives by the same life."[15] The phrase is here put in a different perspective. There is no thought of an extension of the incarnate Christ himself in the church, as if the church stood in direct succession to Christ and inherited his office; it is the *body of Christ* that is extended. It is true that the incarnate Christ cannot be separated from the body of his incarnation—this is the evangelical ambiguity in the term "incarnation." But its evangelical significance is lost if the extension of the body is equated automatically with the extension of the head, and especially if extension is thought of merely in terms of historical succession. Historical succession is an element in the extension, as we have seen; for the incarnation was an event in history, and the church stands in the apostolic succession as the continuing body in which the tradition of the incarnation is preserved and transmitted to

[13] *Inst.*, III, 1. 2; cf. II, 12. 7; III, 11. 10.

[14] This is the real point of his polemic against Osiander in *Inst.*, III, 11. 5.

[15] C. Gore, *The Incarnation of the Son of God*, p. 219. John Murray, 1891.

subsequent generations. But the continuing life of the church as the body of Christ consists in the fact that, as Gore put it, "it embodies the same principle and lives by the same life." Only, this life, by which the church lives, is not a "principle" that the church "embodies" in itself in virtue of its historical succession, however legitimate that may be. The church is constituted the body of Christ, not by the fact that it comes after him, but by the fact that "Christ loved the church and gave himself for her" (Eph. 5:25), and it continues to derive its life from this source. When attention is focused exclusively on the historical relation of the church to Christ, the church seeks to reproduce the source of its life out of the resources of the tradition – and thereby it loses its life.

This was the real issue of the Lutheran Reformation, viz., the source of the church's life. The medieval church had not forgotten what the life of the church is; it knew that the church is the society that is constituted and sustained by forgiveness. Its error was precisely that it had made of forgiveness a "principle" that it "embodied" in itself and that it was itself able to operate. The sacramental system of the medieval church had developed into an elaborate and costly apparatus for the manufacture of forgiveness – but the product had become a shoddy substitute. It was the problem of forgiveness that precipitated Luther's break with Rome; Luther discovered that no ecclesiastically manufactured article can take the place of real forgiveness; for real forgiveness is a miracle and can never be anything other than a miracle; and the word of absolution, *ego te absolvo,* is incredible, unless the *ego* be that of Christ himself.[16] In other words, the "principle" of the church's life, if we may so call the forgiveness by which it coheres, has its sole ground in the original manifestation of life in the Word incarnate, and the fellowship that unites its

[16] It has been noted that even Christ never used this formula but only pronounced men forgiven by God. Cf. Charles Williams, *The Forgiveness of Sins,* p. 59.

members together derives its vitality from the fellowship that Christ has established with us by his incarnate life for us (cf. I John 1:1–3).

The church can be a society of real forgiveness only so long as it continues to receive forgiveness from its real Author; but it cannot do this if it casts itself in the role of successor to Christ and inheritor of his office. The truth, which had been largely forgotten in the medieval church, and which broke through with evangelical—and sometimes explosive—force at the Reformation, is that the Christ who was incarnate continues himself in the mission and work of the Holy Spirit. The Holy Spirit is Christ's gift to the church, but never the possession of the church, never a principle that the church embodies in itself. The church has the Spirit only when it recognizes the Spirit as "The Lord, and Giver of Life,"[17] in whom Christ the Lord continues to represent himself to the church in the power of his incarnate life.

The extension of the incarnation then must be defined as the presence of the Spirit in the church; for the presence of the Spirit is the presence of Christ. Although the mission of the Spirit follows the mission of Christ, it does not supersede it; the incarnation retains the central and decisive place in Christian faith, and the emphasis on the temporal sequence of the two missions, which is so marked in the Paraclete sayings of the Fourth Gospel, is a testimony to that. If the work of Christ must be completed before the Spirit comes, it is because that work is final and sufficient, and the function of the Spirit is to recall and bear witness to it.[18] The presence of the Spirit in the church is attested, accordingly, not by spiritual ecstasies (this is the error which Paul had to combat in the church at Corinth and which has dogged the footsteps of the church throughout its history), but by an articulate confession of the Lordship of Jesus Christ (I Cor. 12:3). And indeed,

[17] Cf. the Nicene Creed.
[18] Cf. *The Holy Spirit in Christian Theology*, pp. 20 ff.

it is by the manner in which he points to the incarnate Christ that the Holy Spirit is identified (I John 4:1–3).

The Holy Spirit, therefore, is more than an endowment of supernatural power bestowed on the church to enable it to discharge the mission that it has inherited from Christ. The mission of the Spirit signifies (1) that without the living presence of Christ himself the church is powerless to do anything (John 15:5); for he alone is the Christ who saves. The gospel is not an impersonal thing that was acquired by Christ and deposited in the church, like a treasure, to be subsequently disbursed by its authorized officers;[19] it is inseparable from Christ himself; its reality is in his incarnate life as the man in whom the forgiveness of God is realized in personal relation with other men. His continued presence in the Spirit with the church is the sole ground and source of forgiveness. (2) The mission of the Spirit also signifies that the realization of the living presence of Christ is solely in his own gift and does not fall under the powers of the church. The Holy Spirit is the Lord, and not the servant, of the church.

The function of the church is described in the New Testament by the term " witness " or " testimony." " Ye shall be witnesses unto me " were Christ's last words spoken on earth to his disciples (Acts 1:8). The term is significant in a number of ways.

In the first place, it clearly indicates the distinction between the church and its Lord. A witness in a court of law is not the principal figure in the case, but a subordinate figure whose function it is to shed light upon the doings of the principal. His task is to direct attention to that other, and not to himself. So the church, as witness to Christ, has, like John the Baptist, to point to its Lord: " Behold the Lamb of God, which taketh away the sin of the world! " (John 1:29). And it cannot do this without, in a measure, effacing itself: " He must increase, but I must decrease " (John 3:30). Indeed, the church must

[19] Cf. Irenaeus, *Against Heresies,* III, 4. 1.

consent to become anonymous; for when it bears testimony that " there is none other name under heaven given among men, whereby we must be saved " (Acts 4:12), it cannot advance its own name beside it.[20]

The term " witness " is also appropriate to the historical nature of the gospel. A witness in a court of law bears witness to something that has happened. The gospel is something that happened; it is the event, or the series of events, that compose the fact of Jesus Christ. And the church's witness to Christ consists, first and foremost, in the narration of the historical events of which he was the subject. The rehearsal of those events formed the fixed core of the primitive apostolic preaching, and it has been stereotyped in the canon of apostolic Scripture on which all later preaching is based. All preaching of the gospel of the incarnation is based ultimately on the text, " And it came to pass." But the recollection of the past, important as that is, is the task of history, and witness means more than history. Even in a court of law the aim is more than the recollection of the past; the aim is the " reconstruction " of what happened, so that it may be made to happen again in the presence of the members of the court. Of course, the reconstruction (which may be aided by pictures and models) is only imaginative. No event of the past can literally be repeated. And this holds true of the event of the incarnation. It is of the essence of evangelical faith that the event of the incarnation is final, decisive, once for all. But just

[20] Cf. I Cor. 1:12–15 and 3:4 ff. A note of caution may be sounded here regarding the current revival of interest in the doctrine of the church, which, although it is to be welcomed in some ways, is not without its dangers. The fact that the doctrine of the church was comparatively late in receiving theological attention is an indication that the church can exist without conscious reflection on its own nature. It would be an error to assume that a high doctrine of the church bespeaks a corresponding reality of the church. An excessive preoccupation with itself may promote a self-consciousness that is as little to be desired in the church as it is in individuals. The church is most truly itself when it is least conscious of itself.

for this reason it is not enough that the event be remembered in the tradition of the church, important though that may be; for it is the event itself that constitutes the gospel, and the tradition concerning it cannot become a substitute for it. The church's preservation of the tradition is an act of witness, whereby it points to the event of the incarnation, not merely with a view to its continued remembrance, but with a view to its becoming reality in the present experience of those to whom it is transmitted.

The church fulfills its witnessing function through "the means of grace," and in these its dual aspect is clearly exhibited. The kerygma, or preaching of the word, consists primarily in the narration of the events that constitute the gospel, but it aims at a "contemporaneous" and decisive confrontation between those events and the hearers to whom they are proclaimed. Communion with Christ—with the real Christ—means participation in the events of his incarnate life. Thus, when the church preaches the birth of Christ, it is not just because this is an event of historical significance which deserves to be commemorated; it is because this event is, literally, "the beginning of the gospel." For the gospel consists in that relation to sinful men upon which Christ entered by being born as man; and the message of Christmas remains in the air unless the first two words of the angelic announcement become true: "*Unto you* is born this day in the city of David a Saviour, which is Christ the Lord" (Luke 2:11). There must be an extension of the incarnation to include us among those *to whom* he is born, and *with whom* he entered into relation. So, in a wondrously involved metaphor, Paul pictures himself to his Galatian readers as being in labor with them until Christ be brought to birth in them (Gal. 4:19). And a German poet has expressed the same point in the familiar lines:

> "Were Christ a thousand times in Bethlehem born,
> And not in thee, thy soul's eternally forlorn."

In the same way, the preaching of the death of Christ, the portrayal of Christ crucified, as Paul calls it (Gal. 3:1), is more than the narration of a past event. The death of Christ has, indeed, its historical finality, its once-for-allness. Having died once, he dies no more (Rom. 6:9 f.). But the life of the church derives from the present reality of the death of Christ; for the death of Christ is the consummation of that personal relation to men in which he lived and in which alone the miracle of the divine forgiveness is present to them. Communion with Christ in his death is the focal point of the church's worship, and it determines the form and pattern of the church's life; for the church lives by participation in the death of Christ (II Cor. 1:5), by being baptized into it (Rom. 6:3), and conformed to it (Rom. 6:5; Phil. 3:10). The preaching of the cross is more than the commemoration of a past event; it is the presentation of Christ crucified as the church's Lord, in relation to whom it has its being.

The real presence of Christ is often associated in a special way with the sacraments. This is legitimate if the word "real" be taken in its strict etymological sense as having reference to the material elements (*res*) of water, bread, and wine, which are used in the sacraments; the real presence of Christ then signifies his presence in the sacraments, in which these material elements are used, as distinguished from his "verbal" presence in preaching, in which only words (*verba*) are used. But if "real" is taken in the accepted modern sense as equivalent to "true" or "genuine," then Christ is really present in both word and sacraments. Confusion between the two connotations has been the source of doctrinal divergence and needless estrangement. The "catholic" tendency to associate the real presence of Christ in an exclusive way with the sacraments, and to exalt the sacraments at the expense of the word, has encouraged the growth of materialistic and magical conceptions of sacramental operation. Against this the "protestant" tendency has been to make the sacraments an appendage to the word and to allow them merely a cognitive significance, as a variant form of the word (visible as distinct from audible), added to assist our feeble powers of comprehension, as pictures are added to the text in children's books. Both positions are one-sided. The weakness of the "protestant" position lies not in the neglect or belittling of the sacraments, of which "catholics" complain, but in the injury it does to the word (contrary to its own better insight) by the assumption that the word has only a cognitive significance, and that as such it forms the standard by which the sacraments are to be measured, forgetting that the standard of reference for both word and sacraments is the measure of the gospel. The word, no less than the sacraments, is a medium of the real presence of Christ. As an Anglican writer has put it, "Preaching, rightly understood, means not preaching about Christ, in the sense of merely recalling the character or teaching of a historical figure, but speaking in such a way that the Holy Spirit can make audible and bring home the Word of God, which is Christ himself, to the minds and consciences of contemporary men and women."[21] Dr. Whale makes the point more explicit when he says, "All Christian preaching finds its only sanction and power in the authority of a human life, death, and resurrection through which God spoke in the fullness of time, and through which, by his Spirit in the church, he speaks so long as time endures."[22] The word preached is an instrument of the Word incarnate, i.e., Christ in the event of his incarnate life; and through it "the original event becomes event all over again through the power of the Spirit, so that in kerygma a man encounters the living Christ, Christ crucified but risen."[23]

It is true, then, to say, with Dr. Whale, that "the sacraments do not add anything to the word."[24] But if this is true, the

[21] A. R. Vidler, *Christian Belief,* p. 79. Charles Scribner's Sons, 1950.

[22] J. S. Whale, *Christian Doctrine,* p. 154. Cambridge University Press, 1941.

[23] T. F. Torrance, in *Scottish Journal of Theology,* 3 (1950), p. 311.

[24] *Op. cit.,* p. 159.

question at once arises, Why are the sacraments added to the word? The answer would seem to be twofold. (1) The conjunction of the sacraments with the word is, to so speak, a reminder to the word of its own true significance as witness to the gospel, which consists, not in words or ideas, but in Christ in the work of his incarnate life. As action performed, the sacrament illustrates the event-character of the gospel, to which the word points. This is the truth in the Reformers' description of the sacrament as the visible word. (2) The addition of the sacraments to the word also serves to demonstrate the inadequacy of all human means to effect the reality of the gospel, to which they point. The sacrament, which begins after the word is finished, shows clearly that the word cannot compass the gospel. But this does not mean that the sacrament is better able to do it. On the contrary, when the church passes from word to sacrament and from speech to action, it is like a man visiting a foreign land who cannot convey his meaning in words, because of his limited knowledge of the language, and who has recourse to signs and gestures. By the presence of the sacrament alongside the word, says Karl Barth, "the church is thereby reminded that all its own words, even when they are blessed and sanctioned by God's word and Spirit, can only aim in the direction of the actual event in which God in his reality encounters man. The visible signs of Baptism and the Lord's Supper have plainly the important function in the life of the church of showing the boundary which lies between what man can say and understand and conceive about God and the inconceivable reality in which God is what he is in himself and for us." [25]

The sacrament of Baptism represents the beginning of the gospel. It corresponds to the baptism of Christ, which is the formal act by which he entered into that relation with humanity in which the gospel consists. Christian baptism marks our introduction into that body which he began to constitute

[25] Karl Barth, *Credo,* pp. 11 f. Kaiser, München, 1935.

by his baptism. It is true, of course, that baptism also presupposes the finished work of Christ, and can thus be interpreted by Paul as baptism into his death (Rom. 6:3). The baptism of Christ was his first step on the road that led to the cross, and he himself spoke of his death as a baptism to be completed (Luke 12:50). But between the beginning and the end there was a road to be traveled, and the gospel was in the traveling of this road. Christian baptism marks the beginning of our Christian life and our entry upon the way by initiation into the body which is constituted by following him who is the Way.

The sacrament of the Lord's Supper represents the end of the gospel; for the death of Christ, which it signifies, was the consummation of that relationship to men upon which he entered at his baptism and in which the gospel of forgiveness is realized. We partake of this sacrament of the end, although we are not yet at the end – indeed, just because we are not yet at the end, because in it we have communion with Christ at his end, i.e., in the power of his finished work, and thereby we are fortified for the continuing journey. In baptism we look back to the beginning, and the church has judged that once this beginning is made, it can never be unmade; therefore baptism is given only once. In the Lord's Supper we look forward to the end; it is pre-eminently the eschatological sacrament, because although we are not yet at the end, we repeatedly reach out after it and seek its power in the present, while we are still on the way.

Controversy over the manner of the real presence of Christ in the sacraments is futile and redundant. The historic controversies presuppose that the question concerns a static presence of Christ in the elements and that it is capable of being answered in terms of a philosophy of substance. This in turn presupposes a view of salvation that was current in the early Greek church, viz., that Christ saves us by his consubstantiality with us. But if, as we have contended, the gospel of the incarnation is to be seen, not in Christ's consubstantiality with us, but in his co-existence with us, if, in other words, Christ saves us, not merely by the constitution of his person, but by the life he lived among us, it is not in the elements, but in the action of the sacraments that his real presence is to be found. The sacraments are actions that represent the historic acts of Christ in his incarnate life.[26] A complete, theoretical-doctrinal exposition of the manner of the real presence is not, therefore, to be expected. It has been pointed out that if we could formulate a doctrine of the sacraments that was entirely satisfying, we could then dispense with the sacraments themselves; for the sacraments are the acts that begin at the point where words fail; they are the acts in which the original, saving acts of Christ "reverberate"[27] in their own key, and they cannot be transposed into the key of systematic doctrine.

The persistent urge to frame a doctrine of the sacrament of the Lord's Supper springs, in part, from a misconception of the sacrament as a sacrifice that the church offers to God, whether it be a literal sacrifice that it offers as an act of propitiation, or a metaphorical sacrifice that it offers as an act of worship. If the sacrament is thus primarily something that the church does, it is intelligible that the church should feel impelled to explain to itself and to others what it does. Now this view of the sacrament presupposes that the original act of Christ, which it "repeats" or "represents," was itself of the nature of a sacrifice that he offered to God. But if, as we have contended, the work of Christ is to be regarded, not as a work of man directed toward God in order to procure his forgiveness, but God's free gift of forgiveness extended to men in the man in whom he enters into personal relation with them at the human level, then the sacrament too must be regarded as a renewal or extension of the gift, and if it is something the church does, the church does it, not because it is able to ex-

[26] Cf. P. T. Forsyth, *The Church and the Sacraments* (3d edit.), pp. 227 ff. Independent Press, 1949.

[27] This was Forsyth's favorite term; *op. cit.*, pp. 231, 233, etc.

plain it, but because it is commanded to do it: "This do in remembrance of me" (I Cor. 11:24); the sacrament is an act of obedience to the grace of God which came by Jesus Christ.

The demand for a doctrine of the sacrament presupposes that the real presence of Christ can be explained in terms of some general principle that can be established independently. Once the general principle is established, the sacrament can be held to effect the real presence of Christ *ex opere operato.* The better mind of the church has been suspicious of this kind of theory and has recognized that if we really have the real presence of Christ in the sacrament, the manner of it is surely unique and *sui generis.* Calvin is a notable example. His was a mind in which the urge to explain was normally uninhibited; but he clearly recognized that in the presence of the sacrament he had reached the limit of explanation. The presence of Christ in the sacrament, he said, is something to be experienced rather than understood.[28] The only answer that can be given to the question how he is present is tautological: he is present sacramentally.

There are, however, two comments that may be added. The tautology is, in effect, a confession that the real presence of Christ in the sacrament is entirely in his own power. It is the work of the Holy Spirit. This is what we mean when we call it a spiritual presence. We do not mean that it is not real. It is real, but its reality is solely the work of the Spirit of Christ. And secondly, the presence of Christ through the Spirit in the sacrament is the real point of eschatology. The point is sometimes missed in the current debate, where it is made to appear as if we had to choose between "realized" and "futurist" eschatology. The truth is that the realized presence of Christ now is the ground of the church's hope in his coming again. The whole life of the church is eschatological; for the source of its life is the continual representation of Christ in the power of his finished work and the promise of his final triumph. The

[28] *Inst.*, IV, 17. 32; cf. §§ 7 and 24.

sacrament is the eschatological bringing-into-the-present of the Christ of the past and of the future, the Christ who suffered under Pontius Pilate and the Christ who shall come to judge the quick and the dead. In the sacrament this Christ, who is the same yesterday and today and for ever, is "known to them in the breaking of the bread" (Luke 24:35). As Dodd says: "Past, present, and future are indissolubly united in the sacrament. It may be regarded as a dramatization of the advent of the Lord, which is *at once* his remembered coming in humiliation and his desired coming in glory, both realized in his true presence in the sacrament."[29] Unless the present life of the church is eschatological in this way, its past is merely archaistic and its future utopian.

There is one further aspect of the church's witness to the gospel that remains to be noticed. We have considered the church's witness as it relates to the word and sacraments, by which it bears witness to the real presence of Christ as the source of its life. But it can bear this witness only as it really lives the life that proceeds from the source; for the real presence of Christ is Christ in the work of his incarnate life bringing the miracle of forgiveness to men in his personal relation to them. The church is the body of Christ, because the life that proceeds from the head flows through the members. The presence of Christ is realized as "an energy of forgiveness in the church."[30] The church bears witness to the miracle of the divine forgiveness by itself venturing to walk on this miraculous element. And the incarnation is extended in the church when the forgiveness that is incarnate in Christ becomes incarnated by his presence in the life of the church.

"The forgiveness of God," wrote H. R. Mackintosh, "is only believable in a certain psychological atmosphere. For that atmosphere two ingredients are essential: first, the living wit-

[29] Dodd, *op. cit.*, p. 94; cf. Cullmann, *Christ and Time*, pp. 73 ff., 154 ff. The Westminster Press, 1950.

[30] Charles Williams, *op. cit.*, p. 65.

ness of pardoned men to the truth in which they themselves have found life and power, and, secondly, the Christian habit of *practising* forgiveness. In other words, the church is not merely a society called to proclaim that loving divine pardon which confronts the penitent alike in the gospel and the sacraments; it is a society in which men are accustomed to forgive each other. The second requisite is as vital as the first. Without it the good news of pardon can make no impression." [31] There can really be no separation here at all. It is not a case of two forgivenesses, which are related to each other as condition and consequence. There is only one forgiveness, and that is the miracle of the forgiveness of God which was brought to men by Christ in his incarnate life and which is continually renewed by his real presence in word and sacraments. It cannot be resolved into a principle; it is always the personal gift of Christ in his incarnation and its extension, and it constitutes his body, of which it is the life. So we are taught to pray, not "Forgive us our debts, *because* we forgive our debtors," nor "Forgive us our debts, *in order that* we may forgive our debtors," but "Forgive us our debts *as* we forgive our debtors." The petition is paraphrased in the Heidelberg Catechism thus: "Be pleased, for the sake of Christ's blood, not to impute to us, miserable sinners, all our transgressions, nor the evil which continues still to cleave to us; as we also find this witness of thy grace in us, that it is our full purpose heartily to forgive our neighbors." [32] The grace to forgive is a witness to the grace by which we are forgiven, because it is the same grace; for there is only one grace, the grace of the Lord Jesus Christ, "who for us men and for our salvation came down from heaven, and was incarnate."

[31] *The Christian Experience of Forgiveness,* pp. 276 f. James Nisbet & Co., Ltd., London, 1927.

[32] Answer to Question 126.

Index